MW01292221

# Discipleship
# for Dummies

By David L. Miner

© 2016, David L. Miner, www.FreedomSiteWriters.com

The **focus** of this book is _Discipleship_ – the process of helping Believers around you to grow in their relationships with God. But the **target** of this book is the Christian with no experience and little to no training in _Discipleship Ministry_, yet who has been given a heart for God such that he or she wants to share with and teach and train others:

to know God;
to know God better; and
to walk with God.

This book is offered to you, with prayers that God will use it to touch the lives of many others through you.  May God bless you in your ministry efforts.

*Every time I think of you, I give thanks to my God. Whenever I pray, I make my requests for all of you with joy, for you have been my partners in spreading the Good News about Christ from the time you first heard it until now. And I am certain that God, who began the good work within you, will continue his work until it is finally finished on the day when Christ Jesus returns. So it is right that I should feel as I do about all of you, for you have a special place in my heart. You share with me the special favor of God, both in my imprisonment and in defending and confirming the truth of the Good News. God knows how much I love you and long for you with the tender compassion of Christ Jesus. I pray that your love will overflow more and more, and that you will keep on growing in knowledge and understanding. For I want you to understand what really matters, so that you may live pure and blameless lives until the day of Christ's return. May you always be filled with the fruit of your salvation—the righteous character produced in your life by Jesus Christ—for this will bring much glory and praise to God.*

[Philippians 1:3-11,NLT]

# Preface

Let's get this out of the way up front. All Scripture is inspired by God and profitable for teaching, rebuking, correcting, and training in righteousness. [see II Timothy 3:16] And I believe that most Modern Translations fall into the category of Scripture, and are honest efforts by honorable people to properly and accurately render the words of God from one language (usually Aramaic or Hebrew or Greek) into a modern language that people can understand, and do it better than other similar efforts. Yet, for many, many Christians around the world, the Authorized Version (authorized by King James, and therefore known by most as the King James Version) remains the standard by which all other efforts are measured. However, I believe that most Modern Translations are up to the implied comparison, and I regularly use a number of translations every time I study the Bible for my own personal edification. In line with that, I have used several translations in this effort. The Authorized Version (KJV), the New Internal Version (NIV) and the New American Standard Version (NASB) are my personal favorites, with cross-references to the Amplified Bible (AMP) and the New Living Translation (NLT) here and there. However, I am not writing this to debate the strengths and merits of various translations; I am writing this to help you grow in your relationship with God, and to help you transfer that growth into others around you. I trust and pray none of these translations used here will prove a problem in your understanding and application of God's Holy Word. I also trust that you will bring your own personal favorite version to this discussion as you work through this book. But more important (more important but _not_ more accurate) than any written version of Scripture is the version of Scripture in your head. Right or wrong, that version controls your actions. So always use the mind God gave you to work through any passage you don't understand until you understand it (in other words, research and study and think and pray until you _DO_ understand each passage), while at the same time referencing the minds God gave other learned men and women by studying the various translations God gave them. Specifically, ONLY GOD has the entire truth. And you have been called by God to "*Study to show thyself approved unto God, a workman that needeth not to be ashamed, rightly dividing the word of truth,*" [II Timothy 2:15, KJV] in order to understand His Truth, and to wisely apply His Truth to your life. Do so with wisdom and understanding, with discernment and good judgment, and with an open heart and mind. We must remember that no translation is "*a matter of one's own interpretation*" [see II Peter 1:20], and that no interpretation will help you grow in wisdom and stature with God and with man unless you allow your heart to discern the truth, and then use your mind to live by that truth. Truth applied is Truth learned.

*"Then you will be able to test and approve what God's will is…"* [Romans 12:2, NIV]

*"…that ye may prove what is that good, and acceptable, and perfect, will of God."* [Romans 12:2, KJV]

*"You therefore, my son, be strong in the grace that is in Christ Jesus. The things which you have heard from me in the presence of many witnesses, entrust these to faithful men who will be able to teach others also."* [II Timothy 2:2, NASB]

# Table of Contents

# Introduction

Discipleship is not a mystery. It is nothing more than your efforts to help other Believers grow in their relationship with God. To put it simply, discipleship is an attempt to help others know Christ, and then to know Christ better, and then to walk with Christ.

If you are currently doing that in any way, you are currently discipling others.

And what we can do together is enhance your ministry. If you have had no training in a discipleship ministry, then you can use this book to increase your effectiveness in discipleship. And if you have had training, or if you are currently using some formal discipleship materials, then this book will supplement those materials.

In this book, we use the *Parable of the Soils*, or what many call the *Parable of the Sower* or the *Parable of the Seed*, to examine some principles of discipleship and to gain some insight into your disciples so you can see what Jesus has told us concerning the spiritual level or maturity of those disciples, and about their receptivity. In that Parable, Jesus tells us about the hearts of your disciples, suggesting that they fall into one of four categories:

- *__Hard Soil__*
  Soil alongside the path that had been packed hard through frequent use. The soil was too hard for the seed to work its way into the soil and sprout. The Word was stolen by Satan before it could sprout or produce fruit.
- *__Rocky Soil__*
  Soil that was never cleared and prepared, that had rocks and other things which restrict the seed from taking root and sprouting. This soil cannot support any real growth when exposed to pressures and persecution, and the plant withers.

- ***Thorny Soil***
  Soil that had possibly been prepared at least a little but still had thorn bushes and other similar impediments, and the seed takes root quickly and begins to grow. But the growth is stunted, affected by many things, and it never grows into much of a plant nor does it produce any real fruit.
- ***Good Soil***
  Good soil that had been properly cleared, plowed, and prepared. The seed takes root, grows well, and produces much fruit .

These are the Soil Types as Jesus presented them. And this book will help you understand the Soil Types and disciple them effectively. If you allow this book to assist you, your disciples will produce fruit.

So, let's get busy and change some lives, shall we?

## Chapter One

# WHAT IS DISCIPLESHIP?

Let me make one thing clear from the beginning. Discipleship IS NOT bugging people concerning the things you do not like about them. Or even about some spiritual failure you see in their lives. That is meddling, and you will make more enemies than friends when you meddle. Maybe you have already discovered this...

Discipleship has been described by many people and in many publications. I cannot and will not attempt to address all those definitions and all those publications. Instead, I am going to adopt and use here what I was taught by Campus Crusade for Christ when I was a student at the University of South Florida in Tampa. And, of course, I am going to slip in some ideas of my own for good measure...

In fact, this might be a good time for me to "slip in" this idea. Your ministry is YOUR MINISTRY! It is established by God and put into practice by you. Your discipleship ministry will be unique to you. You are not required to do what every other discipleship ministry does. You aren't even required to do what this book tells you to do.

What you _ARE_ required to do is be sensitive to the Holy Spirit of God, and to follow what he urges you to do. This is Discipleship Rule Number One! There will be times when you aren't quite sure what he wants you to do. When you face those times, refer back to Rule Number One – be sensitive to the Holy Spirit of God. And in those times of uncertainty concerning your ministry or your disciple, you might just have to rely on what God is doing in you, and then do that with your disciple. I mean, God has been at this for a long time, so you can usually count

1

on what He is doing in you as a reliable pattern for what you can be doing with your disciple.  Not always, but it is a good start.

You see, there is no mandatory definition or pattern or shape or color that one person can claim to be "RIGHT" or "godly" or "the biblical method of discipleship."  As long as you are pursuing Godly character based on Biblical principles, you are engaged in an awesome ministry that will change lives forever.

What I learned from my time ministering with Campus Crusade, and what I have practiced for the 45 years since that time, is really quite simple.  And it is also quite complex.  And it also changes lives!

**Discipleship is a ministry where one Christian (the "discipler") commits to invest into the life of one or more Christians (the "disciple") the concepts and character that God is building into the life of the discipler, and that God WANTS to build into the lives of all of his people.**

A Discipleship Ministry usually involves a specific plan of action, and often involves at least some printed materials to follow.  But please understand that printed materials are always valuable, yet they are not required.  In fact, the original pattern for discipleship we can see in Jesus, and it involved nothing more than walking around and modeling or living the beliefs and the character that he wanted his disciples to learn and then to teach to others.  One does not have to be a "spiritual giant" to disciple others.  But one DOES have to be sincerely following Christ if one expects to see any spiritual growth resulting from the efforts invested in others.

And a couple points of clarification might need to be made here for those who are detail oriented.  There is a difference between being a follower and being a disciple.  There are a number of passages in Scripture that mention or address followers of Jesus, but the passages that address Christ's disciples are usually separate and involve special circumstances or special teaching. For example, Jesus preached to his followers but he sent out his disciples on mission trips. And in one passage, Jesus taught some things that caused most of his "followers" to turn away, leaving only his twelve disciples standing there.

And there is a difference between being a disciple and being an Apostle. Most of the disciples are described in Scripture as Apostles, but not all of them. And most who are described in Scripture as Apostles were also disciples, but not all of them. It seems that Jesus had dozens of close followers and hundreds who followed at a distance. But he specifically called only twelve disciples. And then God appointed even less as Apostles.

Yet we must understand that Scripture never gives us a clear definition of disciple. So I have chosen to use the definition and pattern that I have learned and have seen to be effective in the lives of hundreds of Believers around me.

One more point needs to be made here. You cannot engage in a discipleship ministry where you are building the life of Christ into another person without God doing the same to you. After 45 years engaged in discipleship, possibly the most common source of excitement people have shared with me was the spiritual growth they experienced while discipling others. Let me say this again.

### *Helping others grow helps you grow!*

Allow me to refer you to the story about "the woman at the well" that John described in Chapter Four of his Gospel. I believe there are two distinct messages in this passage, and I have seldom heard anyone address the second message. So I will share it with you since I believe it applies to this ministry of discipleship you are developing.

Pretty much everyone has read or heard how the Samaritan woman was living in adultery and that Jesus discerned this fact without being told. And pretty much everyone has read or heard that the woman was so impressed with Jesus and what he said that she ran off to the village to tell everyone about Jesus. And pretty much everyone has read or heard that the entire village was affected by Jesus as he spent the next several days ministering to them. All that is clear and simple, and I don't need to say anything about that part.

But allow me to share with you what many people have not read or heard.

When Jesus and his disciples first arrived at Jacob's Well, he sat down to rest and sent his disciples into town for some Chinese Takeout. While the Disciples were on the way to get lunch, a woman approached the well. And you know the story. But what is important to us and to discipleship is not the success of Christ's evangelism methods. What is important to us here and now is the story about what happened AFTER Jesus spoke with the woman.

As the woman was leaving her encounter with Jesus and heading back into town, the disciples returned from their mission to get lunch. As they spread out the food for everyone to eat, some of the disciples noticed that Jesus was not eating. So they did the natural thing, and they urged him to eat. His response was important for us to understand.

*But he said to them, "I have food to eat that you know nothing about."* [John 4:32, NIV]

The disciples immediately wondered how Jesus could have eaten while they were on their lunch run. I am pretty sure they were convinced that *Domino's* did not deliver that far from town. So they were more than a little confused. But Jesus never explained what he meant. Instead, he left it for the disciples to discover what he meant. And he left it for you and me to discover what he meant.

Jesus was stating (without explanation) a spiritual principle that you may have already discovered in your own life. If not, you will discover it as you develop your Discipleship Ministry. Simply put, when you minister to others, you are spiritually fed by the Holy Spirit. You feel fulfilled and enhanced and empowered in ways that nothing else can match.

As you disciple others, God will change your life to be more like him.

Count on it. Expect it. Plan for it. And watch how the Holy Spirit of God changes your life while he helps you change the lives of others.

**The Ministry of the Holy Spirit in this world revolves around three issues:**
*-to know Jesus*
*-to know Jesus better*
*-to know and live like Jesus has already won this war*

## Chapter Two

# THE ROLE OF JUDGING IN DISCIPLESHIP

You have probably heard it said often, "God helps those who help themselves." And since this is said so frequently by both Christians and non-Christians alike, modern Christianity has sort of developed an entire theology around this claim.

Christian Self-Help groups, ministries, and even some churches devote themselves to the belief that "God helps those who help themselves," and we see lots of books and activities and recently entire belief systems consumed with helping Believers see how to help themselves, how to feel better about themselves, how to experience "all God has for us." We are told by these people and these ministries how much God wants us to be happy here on earth so we should go around and _CLAIM_ the material things we want and the "spiritual" goals we set so that God knows what to give us to make us happy.

It would be better if these ministries and churches and church leaders would devote themselves to _understanding_ Scripture and then _teaching_ Scripture, rather than _using_ Scripture to promote their belief systems.

But much of modern Christianity has become lazy and greedy, and we often don't use biblical discernment and sound judgment. Instead, God and his Church have seen an entire generation of Christians become spiritually neutered because they have taken to heart slogans, catch-phrases, sound bites, and biblical buzzwords similar to that one above. You have probably heard of "pop psychology;" I submit that we have developed an entire generation of "pop Christianity" where something that makes sense in a logical world MUST be true in the Spiritual world. This has polluted our theology and modified our thinking in non-biblical ways.

***In no way is this "pop Christianity" mindset more manifest than in the issues of judging others.***

"Who are you to judge me?" has become common in our television programs and in our movies. Even Christians have adopted the mantra of "don't judge, just love" in an effort to bring more people into our churches.

Coaches are *required* to judge athletes and their weaknesses. Bosses are *required* to judge applicants in light of the company's needs, and employees in light of their actions and accomplishments. Teachers are *required* to judge students to see if they have learned enough to be promoted to the next grade.

But Christians are somehow and for some reason *forbidden* to judge others!

It is reasoned that one cannot lead without first judging and deciding who could best assist you in leadership responsibilities. Yet we are told by secular and spiritual leaders alike that we cannot judge others. ["*Do not judge, or you too will be judged.*" Matthew 7:1, NIV] So we decide we cannot turn to God for good moral judgment and discernment of others, and we are left with developing secular management techniques that allow us to help others to "rise above the crowd" so we can select without judging. As a result we often select our spiritual associates and assistants <u>not</u> for their hearts for and walks with God but instead according to which ones manifest more strengths consistent with our needs. Instead of measuring the godly character and the wisdom of one's heart for God, we use secular techniques to sort through some list of candidates. We seldom get inside the other person; seldom learn what makes them tick and what motivates them; seldom clearly see their strengths and their flaws. This usually means we are sooner or later going to be disappointed with them, or they do not last long, because we never properly and adequately judged their heart for God in the first place. This strategy might work in a

7

large and godless corporation, but it will never work in a ministry led by God's Holy Spirit.

Last year I met a man in prison and quickly became bonded to him. He had a heart for God that truly inspired me, and he showed this heart in circumstances that would cause most Christians to cower in the corner, intimidated into silence. As we got to know each other over the next month or so, he showed me his strong desire to help Christian men grow in their relationships with God. But he confessed the absence of any experience or church training that would prepare him for this discipleship ministry, and because of this he had no idea how to go about ministering to others. He related an experience early in his attempts at ministry where he was trying to help another prisoner gain an insight into the character of Jesus and how to manifest that character in a world needing to see Jesus. But the man strongly objected to something said by my friend. *"You are judging me! You have no right to judge me! Jesus said for you to not judge people, and you have violated the words of Jesus!"* The man then walked away from my friend to never seek him out again.

It was clear that my friend was deeply moved by this experience, and not in a good way. And it was also clear that my friend had no idea how he was to teach and train and disciple others without judging them in some way. So my friend turned to me in his turmoil for answers about discipling others without judging. His agony made me think more about what the Bible had to say about discipleship, and especially about judging, than I had ever before considered. This book was written for him. Ray or Roy, I have forgotten his name – this book is dedicated to you and your heart for discipleship.

I recently read in an excellent fiction novel written by an author I truly enjoy where a pediatrician at an inner city free clinic thought something like, "I am not judging anyone, and I try to not let them see my true feelings on their issues and situations." The context of this mental comment was a full paragraph of text where the pediatrician explained to himself that teen sexual activities and teen pregnancy and single-parent inner city families all have horrible consequences, but he just the same tried to not show anything other than encouragement to his patients. He equated being outwardly positive with being non-judgmental. The comment was simply a single line in an entire book, not given any importance at all. In fact, the comment was dismissed by the main character in the book in such a way that made it clear the character (and presumably the author) believed the comment was really no big deal; of no real significance at all.

But this fictional man was lying to himself, or else the author was lying to his readers. The doctor in the story was clearly judging, obvious because he tried to hide his true feelings. He was clearly judging, obvious because the diseases and addictions and abuses he saw and dealt with each and every day were things he fervently prayed his children and others would *NEVER* experience. He was clearly judging the decisions and the resulting experiences of his many patients as being terrible, and resulting in terrible consequences. In truth, he was *WAS* judging them and he just didn't want the people to *KNOW* he was judging them.

Most of us have had a similar experience, and many of us have it regularly. We see bad actions and bad results and bad people on a frequent, maybe daily, basis. But based on the words of Jesus in the 7th chapter of Matthew and the 6th chapter of Luke, and other Scripture passages, we have become convinced that judging them is wrong and bad; that judging is somehow in itself sin. So we tell ourselves and maybe others that we are not judging anyone.

Yet we naturally judge them, and we just don't want anyone to *know* we are judging.

Believers have been taught that this same loathing of judgment must serve as the basis for all our dealings with unbelievers. We have been taught that we must never let the unbeliever ever see any judgment on our part of their actions, attitudes, or beliefs. And this refusal to show any judgment in any way has resulted in Churches and Church Leaders opening their doors to homosexuals and alcoholics and idolaters and all sorts of people who practice what the Bible condemns, while allowing these sinners, these practitioners of actions the Bible so clearly condemns, to feel comfortable in their sins to the extent that we don't call them out of their sins.

This is a good thing – it is good that we make these people feel accepted before Jesus.

**But it is not good for ANYONE that we make these people feel comfortable enough <u>with</u> their sins that they remain <u>in</u> their sins! Not good for the Kingdom of Heaven, or for the people going to that Kingdom, or for the people NOT going to that Kingdom.**

No one experiences any benefit **<u>at all</u>** from a false condemnation of judging, which leads to a false tolerance of sin, which usually leads to a false comfort with sin!

On the other hand, how do we avoid allowing them to feel comfortable enough to remain in their sins unless we judge them? And how can we judge them without offending them or condemning them or offending other Believers, or in some other way feeling or looking like we have failed Scripture when it seems to offer two apparently contradictory but equally impossible concepts? *"Do not judge lest ye be judged also."* [Matthew 7:1, KJV] And, *"All have sinned and fall short of the glory of God."* [Romans 3:23, NIV]

It is usually true that a Christian would want to communicate God's love and acceptance to another person who is in some kind of need, but without seeming to reject them. Jesus himself showed us many times how to accept people in the midst of their sins. Yet not once in Scripture do we ever see Jesus masking his hatred for and judgment of sin. Instead, he confronted sin every day. For example, it was his frequent practice to heal someone and then challenge him or her to "Go and sin no more." He usually did so gently and lovingly, but he did so quite clearly.

His meeting the Samaritan woman at Jacob's Well, described in chapter 4 of the Gospel of John, is a classic example of Jesus loving and accepting the individual while judging and condemning her sin. Christ starts the conversation with an innocent request - "Will you give me something to drink?" He moves into comments of such depth that she is compelled to respond. As they engage in what is obviously a spiritual discussion, Jesus follows the social custom of the day and suggests she get her husband so he can join in, participate in their discussion. She admits she has no husband, and Jesus responds with the claim that she has had five husbands and is currently living with a man to whom she is not married. This is a clear accusation of adultery, a sin which required death in Jewish Law.  Yet Jesus pointed out her sin in a gentle and loving way that drew her in rather than rejecting her.  And rather than making her feel rejected and condemned, she felt so positive about being confronted with her sin that she went into town and brought a group of friends to hear what Jesus had to say.  The end result of this confrontation was that Jesus spent a couple days in town sharing the Gospel with the entire village.

Clearly, Jesus knew how to love and accept a person. And clearly, Jesus was not afraid of confronting sin.  And just as clearly, Jesus knew how to love the sinner without accepting the sin.

Some years ago, I was approached by a man who asked me if I would help him find some answers to some questions he had about the Bible. I am always looking for opportunities to talk about Jesus and his biography, so I eagerly assented. And the man got right to the heart of his issue within seconds.  He asked me if homosexuality was really the horrible sin that so many Christians claimed. We talked about homosexuality for several minutes, and looked at some passages from the Bible that addressed the issue. When I read to him the passage in chapter 1 of Romans, where the writer suggested that homosexual acts are "unnatural" and a "perversion," our discussion transitioned from a friendly chat about what the Bible teaches to something quite negative. At that point, the man got very offensive, and said in an aggressive manner, "But doesn't the Bible tell you not to judge? Aren't you sinning by judging me? You have no right to judge me!" My response came without any thought on my part, which often is not a good thing. I replied in what I hoped was a gentle and accepting voice, "Please don't misunderstand me. I am not judging you at all. I never even said you were a homosexual or that you were going to Hell for it. But when it comes to homosexual activities, I don't HAVE to judge anything. God has already judged homosexuality, and he calls it a perversion. I am merely sharing with you what God has already said about the issue. If you have a problem with that, you don't have a problem with me – you have a problem with God!" The man paused for a few seconds and then walked away without a word.

I could have been more gentle in my response, and even tried to make the man feel more comfortable with his homosexuality, but I did not. And maybe I would have had the man not been so aggressive in his claim that I was sinning by judging him. But I think I would still have made the same point.

*What God has already judged as sin is clearly and eternally sin, and I don't need to judge it at all.*

Please understand this concept. When the Word of God clearly refers to actions and attitudes as sin, I don't need to judge those actions and attitudes. All I need do is pass along **God's judgments** of those actions and activities. I am not judging those actions and activities if all I am doing is passing on God's words.

What God has already judged is judged for all eternity!

While Christians may need to be gentle and sensitive and wise when we pass on these and other passages; while we may need to learn how to "love the sinner while hating the sin;" while we may need to learn to love others the way Jesus loved them, *we never need to accept sin!*

### The trick is to love the sinner AND hate the sin!

The ONLY alternative will result in everyone somehow accepting sin, somehow allowing everything to be seen as equally good. And that alternative will defeat godliness every time. That alternative will profane the death of Jesus more than 2,000 years ago!

KNOW THIS! You cannot pursue God without pursuing holiness. And you can't pursue holiness without rejecting sin. And you cannot reject sin without first labeling it as sin. And you cannot label it sin without judging it as wrong.

## *Judging is a necessary part of being a Christian.*

So why is it considered so wrong to judge someone? I submit to you that it is the current political and social attempt to create a totally amoral world that is behind the almost universal condemnation of judging others. But that it best left for another article...

So what makes the act of assessing the goodness or the rightness or badness or wrongness of an action or of a person, in a social or spiritual sense, unacceptable? And what passages in *God's Word* support this conclusion?

When the Bible says, "*Judge not lest you be judged,*" what does it mean?

The belief that it is wrong to judge someone often leads Christians to a verbal claim that we are NOT judging anyone. And this verbal claim that we are not judging anyone is usually an introduction to a watered-down presentation of biblical claims or biblical standards. After all, how can we present the life, death and resurrection of Jesus as God's plan for a sinful world without addressing sin? How can we speak of sin or of godliness without looking like we are suggesting that someone might be sinning or should be more godly? This attempt at diluting the Word of God so we won't be accused of judging anyone has led many to a powerless and empty presentation of God's call on all Believers to be holy and Christ-like. And any presentation of the need for atonement requires at least an admission of, if not a presentation of, sin!

Christians cannot have a powerful and positive impact on the Believers and unbelievers around them without taking a clear and powerful stand against sin. Scripture makes that very clear. If we communicate that sin is somehow acceptable, even if for only a short time, we imply that Jesus died for nothing and we insult his sacrifice and memory.

Yet any examples of taking a stand for Christ and against sin that we see or hear about often resemble a large sign in the front yard exclaiming the world must *"Turn Or Burn!"* Almost every television show and Hollywood movie presents Biblical Christianity as stupid and obnoxious and useless and condemning and clearly something no highly-evolved human would desire to know, much less hang around. But there are options... Believers can take a clear stand against sin without conforming to those offensive and inaccurate descriptions.

I submit that in our paranoid attempt to appear as non-judgmental Christians, we have instead sold out our Lord and Savior. We cannot talk about sin and the world's need for a Savior without taking a moral and spiritual stand. And many of us have drawn back from taking that stand for fear of being accused of being judgmental. The world needs a Savior and many Christians fear saying that!

*"For all have sinned and fall short of the glory of God,"* [Romans 3:23] is a judgment from God!

*"There is no one righteous, not even one,"* [Romans 3:10] is no casual statement!

*"You shall be holy for I am holy,"* [I Peter 1:16] is not a recommendation!

*"...He has reconciled you by Christ's physical body through death to present you holy in His sight,"* [Colossians 1:23] was not an optimistic dream!

*"...He chose us in Him before the creation of the world to be holy and blameless in his sight,"* [Ephesians 1:4] was not a reference to some Plan B!

The truth is simple - God expects us to be holy and Christ-like; perhaps less so in our early years as a Christian, but definitely more so in our later years. But are we expected to be

Christ-like based SOLELY on our consciences? Are other Christians expected to live and minister around us and yet keep quiet about the weaknesses and shortcomings they see in us? Does God expect our spiritual leaders to ONLY offer us encouragement and kudos? Is God's cause best served when we ignore suggestions from others that we believe are "judging" us? Can we benefit from the "iron sharpens iron" effects of being in relationship with other Believers if we ONLY listen for and allow comments that we consider to be positive and non-judgmental?

Joel Osteen in his ministry offers a resounding YES to these questions.

Dr. Arnold Prater, a preacher and teacher with the small denomination in which I grew up, said something in a sermon I heard almost 50 years ago which has made such an impact on me that it has stuck with me through all these years. He said, *"It is a curse for a Christian to be indistinguishable from a good moral person."* In his sermon, Dr. Prater was teaching that Believers are called to a holy and Christ-like life, and that this holy and Christ-like life is supernatural in nature and can never be mistaken for being merely a good moral life.

So the question must be answered, *"How does one grow into such a life, and become so Christ-like, that one cannot be mistaken for being merely a good moral person?"*

Clearly and obviously, the Holy Spirit plays a primary role in our growth and learning.

*"But when He, the Spirit of Truth, comes, He will guide you into all truth."* [John 16:13, NIV]

*Being confident of this very thing, that he which hath begun a good work in you will perform it until the day of Jesus Christ...* [Philippians 1:6, KJV]

But just as clearly, Scripture declares that we Christians are to teach and instruct each other in all issues of life and godliness.

*"It was he who gave some to be apostles, some to be prophets, some to be evangelists, and some to be pastors and teachers, to prepare God's people for works of service, so that the Body of Christ may be built up until we all reach unity in the faith and in the knowledge of the Son of God and become mature, attaining to the whole measure of the fullness of Christ."* [Ephesians 4:9-13, NIV]

*"Till I come, give attendance to reading, to exhortation, to doctrine."* [I Timothy 4:13, KJV]

*"And the things you have heard me say in the presence of many witnesses entrust to reliable men who will also be qualified to teach others."* [II Timothy 2:2, NIV]

*"All scripture is given by inspiration of God, and is profitable for doctrine, for reproof, for correction, for instruction in righteousness: That the man of God may be perfect, thoroughly furnished unto all good works."* [II Timothy 3:16-17, KJV]

The entire concept of "iron sharpening iron" found in Proverbs 27:17 _presumes and demands_ interaction between people where someone is judging. And all of Chapter 2 in Titus gets very specific in the details of what issues and concepts need to be taught to, and expected of, people who want to follow Jesus.

Paul himself "goes from preaching to meddling" in almost every one of his Epistles, telling this one to use his gift more and these two to cease striving and be reconciled and that one to cease from certain actions or activities. Paul even tells an entire church that they should each one be embarrassed that no one had addressed and rejected a man engaged in specific sexual sin that was well-known to everyone in that particular church.

So is "judging" to be allowed only from the biblical authors? Or is it to be allowed from the preacher? Or is it to be allowed from our Elders? Or is it to be allowed from our parents? Or is it to be allowed from our friends?

Is it possible to teach, train, and disciple other Believers without appearing as if one is judging them?

And what does "judging" truly mean? Why does one passage seem to tell us to not judge others, and then another passage seem to call us to teach and correct and reprove each other?

It will help us if we understand the Greek words used by the Biblical authors in the many different passages which we read and possibly use when we study and discuss this controversial issue of judging. Where a Biblical author might use one of several Greek words, our English translators end up using only one - *judge*. To know which Greek word, even which tense of which Greek word, is used by the original author allows us to understand more clearly what the Bible actually teaches about judging.

In Matthew 7:1, we read the words of Jesus:

*"Do not judge, or you too will be judged. For in the same way you judge others, you will be judged, and with the measure you use, it will be measured to you."* [Matthew 7:1, NIV]

We read similar prohibitions in Romans 2, but they are more complete and maybe even more condemning:

*"You, therefore, have no excuse, you who pass judgment on someone else, for at whatever point you judge the other, you are condemning yourself, because you who pass judgment do the same things. Now we know that God's judgment against those who do such things is based on truth. So, when you, a mere man, passes judgment on them and yet do the same things, do you think you will escape God's judgment?"* [Romans 2:1-4, NIV]

*Therefore you have no excuse, everyone of you who passes judgment, for in that which you judge another, you condemn yourself; for you who judge practice the same things. And we know that the judgment of God rightly falls upon those who practice such things. But do you suppose this, O man, when you pass judgment on those who practice such things and do the same yourself, that you will escape the judgment of God? Or do you think lightly of the riches of His kindness and tolerance and patience, not knowing that the kindness of God leads you to repentance?* [Romans 2:1-4, NASB]

In both passages, the Biblical authors use the same Greek word - *krino.* Gr-*krino* means to judge, to condemn, to damn; and it was used by the writers throughout the *New Testament* to indicate a situation where someone determines that an individual is destined for hell based on external actions or internal attitudes, which would lead us to simplistic and incomplete discernment. And Gr-*krino* is taken to an extreme when we Gr-*catakrino* others, when we judge against others as deserving hell.

Yes, the Bible does _tell_ us that we should not judge others. And it _means_ that humans do not have the insight or the authority to judge another as being bound for heaven or hell just based on external actions or perceived internal attitudes. So if we **presume** to Gr-*krino* others as destined for Hell because they act or speak in a certain way which SEEMS inconsistent with our understanding of a true heart for God, then we risk God using that same superficial measuring stick the next time we lie or gossip or swear or slip into _any_ of the unrighteous thoughts or actions that many of us commit.

Now, go back and look at the context of those two warnings - Matthew 7 and Romans 2.

In chapter 7 of Matthew, we see Jesus in the middle of the longest single discourse of his ministry, as far as we know. And who was Jesus teaching? At that point in time, we know that the public ministry of Jesus was becoming well-known and well-respected and incredibly popular. People gathered around Jesus wherever he walked just to hear him and his teachings. In that particular situation reported in the Gospel according to Matthew, there was a crowd gathering around Jesus in town, and he wanted to spend some time teaching his disciples. So *"he went up on a mountainside and sat down. His disciples came to him, and he began to teach them, saying..."* [Matthew 5:1-2, NIV] What Christians usually call the *"Sermon on the Mount"* was a long teaching session that Jesus had intended for his disciples. Others may have overheard, and even benefited, but Jesus clearly intended the teaching for his disciples.

And in that teaching session, Jesus covered an entire series of concepts and issues, most of them related to spiritual measuring sticks. By that I mean that Jesus gave his disciples a stack of rulers that could be used to measure one's spiritual maturity and spiritual growth. Some of these rulers involved specific actions, but most of those measuring sticks involved internal attitudes. And in the midst of all this, Jesus warned his disciples that they could not judge if someone is headed for hell [Gr – krino] simply based on certain external actions and internal attitudes. Jesus went on to state that the simplistic and incomplete ruler they used to pronounce condemnation on others will be used on them, and he indicated that none of them or us would fare well under those criteria.

The *Sermon on the Mount* contains many different criteria that he intended his disciples to use in determining spiritual maturity, their own and others, and he _expected_ them to use those criteria in their respective ministries. And in the midst of this teaching about measuring people's spiritual maturity, Jesus explained that these spiritual measuring sticks COULD be used to discern spiritual maturity and spiritual growth, but COULD NOT be used to discern whether or not someone was saved or going to hell!

The disciples of Christ could not GR-*krino* anyone without running a severe risk to themselves!

We see something similar in the book of Romans. The last half of the first chapter of Romans we see Paul laying out what I call the "steps to depravity." Paul tells us how mankind, individually and collectively, chooses to walk down a path of rejecting God. This path contains seven steps, from the slightly naughty to the severely evil. The end result of this path is a long list of sins.

> *"They have become filled with every kind of wickedness, evil, greed and depravity. They are full of envy, murder strife, deceit and malice. They are gossips, slanderers, God-haters, insolent, arrogant and boastful; they invent ways of doing evil; they disobey their parents; they are senseless, faithless, heartless, ruthless. Although they know God's righteous decree that those who do such things deserve death, they not only continue to do these things but also approve of those who practice them."*
> [Romans 1:29-32, NIV]

This is indeed a bad report card!

And these actions and attitudes, as a whole, are reflected by those without Christ, as a whole. I doubt that any given sinner is guilty of each and every item on the list. But if you list all unbelievers, and then list all the transgressions performed by all those unbelievers, you would see this list.

And Paul tells us to not JUDGE (Gr-*krino*) those who perform transgressions on the list as deserving hell! Why? Because almost all Christians are guilty of gossiping! Almost all Believers are guilty of envy, strife, deceit and many others on the list. So, Paul says, if you are going to use this list of transgressions to condemn someone to hell, then by that same criteria, you are also destined for hell, *". . .because you who pass judgment do the same things."* [Romans 2:1, NIV]

So it is clear that the Word of God commands Believers to NOT proclaim anyone's eternal destiny based on external activities and perceived internal attitudes. Christians are not to judge (Gr-*krino* - a verb) others, which would result in those

20

others receiving judgment (Gr-*krisis* - a noun), meaning someone is accused, condemned, and damned to an eternity in Hell.

There are, however, variations on the use of this word which are usually translated into the English word for judge, too, but which really mean "to investigate or scrutinize" [Gr-*anakrino*] or "to discriminate or distinguish" [Gr-*diakrino*]. The root word and its several variations are often translated into the same English word for judge, but their meanings are so clearly different. It is the root [Gr-*krino*] that we are forbidden to do. But it is the variations on that root [Gr-*anakrino* and Gr-*diakrino*] which Scripture demands that we practice, and that we practice them with wisdom.

> *We have not received the spirit of the world but the Spirit who is from God, that we may understand what God has freely given us. This is what we speak, not in words taught us by human wisdom but in words taught by the Spirit, expressing spiritual truths in spiritual words. The man without the Spirit does not accept the things that come from the Spirit of God, for they are foolishness to him, and he cannot understand them, because they are spiritually discerned. The spiritual man makes judgments about all things, but he himself is not subject to any man's judgment...* [I Corinthians 2:12-15, NIV]

Here, Paul is telling Believers that we judge-scrutinize-examine-discern all things to understand their spiritual value and what we should or should not do with them.

But then Paul goes further in that same Epistle:

> *It is actually reported that there is immorality among you, and immorality of such a kind as does not exist even among the Gentiles, that someone has his father's wife. You have become arrogant and have not mourned instead, so that the one who had done this deed would be removed from your midst. For I, on my part, though absent in body but present in spirit, have already judged him who has so*

*committed this, as though I were present. In the name of our Lord Jesus, when you are assembled, and I with you in spirit, with the power of our Lord Jesus, I have decided to deliver such a one to Satan for the destruction of his flesh, so that his spirit may be saved in the day of the Lord Jesus. Your boasting is not good. Do you not know that a little leaven leavens the whole lump of dough? Clean out the old leaven so that you may be a new lump, just as you are in fact unleavened. For Christ our Passover also has been sacrificed. Therefore let us celebrate the feast, not with old leaven, nor with the leaven of malice and wickedness, but with the unleavened bread of sincerity and truth. I wrote you in my letter not to associate with immoral people; I did not at all mean with the immoral people of this world, or with the covetous and swindlers, or with idolaters, for then you would have to go out of the world. But actually, I wrote to you not to associate with any so-called brother if he is an immoral person, or covetous, or an idolater, or a reviler, or a drunkard, or a swindler—not even to eat with such a one. For what have I to do with judging outsiders? Do you not judge those who are within the church? But those who are outside, God judges. Remove the wicked man from among yourselves.* [I Corinthians 5:1-12, NASB]

And here, Paul is chastising an entire church of Believers because they DID NOT judge or scrutinize or evaluate the spiritual impact (*"Do you not know that a little leaven leavens the whole lump of dough?"*) of a series of actions performed by a member of that local Body of Christ.

The Body of Christ, ALL CHRISTIANS, are expected by God to judge other Believers!

*Him that is weak in the faith receive ye, but not to doubtful disputations. For one believeth that he may eat all things: another, who is weak, eateth herbs. Let not him that eateth despise him that eateth not; and let not him which eateth not judge him that eateth: for God hath received him. Who art thou that judgest another man's servant? to his own master he standeth or falleth. Yea, he shall be holden up: for God is able to make him stand. One man esteemeth one day above another: another esteemeth every day alike. Let every man be fully persuaded in his own mind. He that regardeth the day, regardeth it unto the Lord; and he that regardeth not the day, to the Lord he doth not regard it. He that eateth, eateth to the Lord, for he giveth God thanks; and he that eateth not, to the Lord he eateth not, and giveth God thanks. For none of us liveth to himself, and no man dieth to himself. For whether we live, we live unto the Lord; and whether we die, we die unto the Lord: whether we live therefore, or die, we are the Lord's. For to this end Christ both died, and rose, and revived, that he might be Lord both of the dead and living. But why dost thou judge thy brother? or why dost thou set at nought thy brother? for we shall all stand before the judgment seat of Christ.* [Romans 14:1-10, KJV]

*Now accept the one who is weak in faith, but not for the purpose of passing judgment on his opinions. One person has faith that he may eat all things, but he who is weak eats vegetables only. The one who eats is not to regard with contempt the one who does not eat, and the one who does not eat is not to judge the one who eats, for God has accepted him. Who are you to judge the servant of another? To his own master he stands or falls; and he will stand, for the Lord is able to make him stand. One person regards one day above another, another regards every day alike. Each person must be fully convinced in his own mind. He who observes the day, observes it for the Lord, and he who eats, does so for the Lord, for he gives thanks to God; and he who eats not, for the Lord he does not eat, and gives thanks to God. For not one of us lives for himself, and not one dies for himself; for if we live, we live for the Lord, or if we die, we die for the Lord; therefore whether we live or die, we are the Lord's. For to this end Christ died and lived again, that He might be Lord both of the dead and of the living. But you, why do you judge your brother? Or you again, why do you regard your brother with contempt? For we will all stand before the judgment seat of God.* [Romans 14:1-10, NASB]

Here we see Paul calling us to discern which Believers are strong in their faith, and which ones are weak, so we can avoid offending the weak Believers.

*So what ARE Christians called to do with regards to confronting sin and encouraging growth within the Body of Christ and outside the Body of Christ?*

I submit that there are three separate issues here, based on the audience: Believers confronting non-Believers, Believers confronting Believers, and Believers in a position of some spiritual authority confronting those under their spiritual ministry and care. And perhaps we can see a guideline or instruction in how to approach these different groups from Scripture itself. (*Imagine that!*)

In the 16th chapter of the Gospel of John, we see Jesus teaching about the ministry of the Holy Spirit.

*"And when he comes, he will convict the world concerning sin, righteousness, and judgment. Concerning sin because the world does not know me; concerning righteousness because I go to the Father and you no longer behold me; concerning judgment because the ruler of this world has been judged."*
[John 16:8-11, NIV]

Here we see that Jesus is telling us of the three primary categories into which all actions by the Holy Spirit in this world fall. This passage does not declare with certainty that the Holy Spirit does not accomplish anything else in this world, but the words Jesus uses seem to *imply* that very assertion. This is what the Holy Spirit *DOES* in this world, and if our respective ministries are directed by the Holy Spirit, then our ministries will reflect his ministry.

In other words, Jesus is pointing out three different groups with three different needs, and shows how the Holy Spirit will meet those three separate needs. And Jesus is implying that Spirit-led Believers will do the same.

Taken literally, the Holy Spirit's actions with regard to an unbelieving world [Gr-*cosmos*] that does not know Jesus does *not* involve telling sinners that specific sins are indeed sins. His ministry to unbelievers relates to helping them see that they do not know Jesus and need to know Jesus. The Holy Spirit deals with sinners *"...concerning sin because they do not know me,"* according to the words of Jesus. If we take this at face value, sermons on the evils of alcohol or gambling, discussions on how pornography is sin, and presentations of WWJD are a waste of time, when directed at unbelievers. It is not their SINS that the Holy Spirit deals with, but their SINFULNESS! Seriously, if someone does not know Jesus, how in the world will they know what Jesus would do in any given circumstance? And why would they care?

As Paul clarified to us, we have a ministry of reconciliation with regards to unbelievers.

> *All this is from God, who reconciled us to himself through Christ and gave us the ministry of reconciliation: that God was reconciling the world to himself in Christ, not counting men's sins against them. And he has committed to us the message of reconciliation. We are therefore Christ's ambassadors, as though God were making his appeal through us. We implore you on Christ's behalf: Be reconciled to God.* [II Corinthians 5:18-20, NIV]

Sinners have one need and the Holy Spirit will focus on that one need - *to know Jesus*. If we are living a holy and righteous life, there are unbelievers around us who are watching us and seeing their need of Jesus.

> *Therefore, since we are surrounded by such a great cloud of witnesses, let us throw off everything that hinders and the sin that so easily entangles, and let us run with perseverance the race marked out for us. Let us fix our eyes on Jesus, the author and perfecter of our faith, who for the joy set before him endured the cross, scorning its shame, and sat down at the right hand of the throne of God. Consider him who endured such opposition from sinful men, so that you will not grow weary and lose heart.*
> [Hebrews 12:1, NASB]

While this passage in Hebrews seems to be discussing past Believers watching present Believers, I believe the concept applies to both Believers and unbelievers watching us all the time. The witnesses around us, both Believers and unbelievers, are being drawn to Christ as long as we are living in Christ. But they are being drawn toward two different objectives. We again need to remember these objectives: 1) to know Jesus, and 2) to know Jesus better. The Holy Spirit uses our lives to draw unbelievers to Jesus, and to draw Believers *closer* to Jesus.

*The Holy Spirit doesn't point unbelievers to their SINS. He points unbelievers to their SINFULNESS, and then he points them to Jesus.*

Know this - if we live like Jesus wants us to live, then the Holy Spirit is hard at work around us drawing sinful people to God.

And if our ministries point unbelievers to Jesus, we really won't need to judge (*Gr-krino*) anyone. Unbelievers will come to us and ask about God because the Holy Spirit is at work prompting them to ask. The question might be disguised; the unbeliever may not realize he or she is asking about God. But the opportunity will be there to tell him or her about God because the Holy Spirit is using our lives to draw them to God. If the Holy Spirit is not using our lives to point unbelievers to God, then it is because our lives are falling far short of what Jesus wants for us and promises to us. Your life doesn't have to be perfect for the Holy Spirit to use you, but it does have to be submitted to Him.

The second group of people that the Holy Spirit targets is Believers. Here the ministry efforts are exclusively to point us to Jesus for our example of holiness and righteous living. Jesus tells us that when he goes to Heaven, *"you no longer behold me."* When he is no longer living in front of us, we no longer have a living example of how to live. So the Holy Spirit will point us to Jesus and call us to live like Him.

Know this - the Holy Spirit does not convict Believers of sin; he convicts Believers of Christ's righteousness and gives us the desire to live like Him, and the power to do so.

No matter how many times we hear the saying, I can find no place in Scripture where it tells us that the Holy Spirit "convicts a Believer of sin" or where he focuses Christians on sins in the Believer's life. The Holy Spirit would rather point us to Christ and to Christ's righteousness than He would point us toward our sins and Satan's short but possibly important victory in our lives. We might FEEL like the Holy Spirit is pointing to our sin, but that is merely the REACTION of our conscience and our spirit when the Holy Spirit points us toward the righteousness of Christ.

***There is nothing about the Holy Spirit that points us toward Satan; He is too busy pointing us toward Jesus.***

This is not to say that God does not deal with our sin, nor can we say that the Biblical authors chose to ignore specific sins. What we can take away from this is the fact that the Holy Spirit points Believers to Jesus as the *means* of dealing with our sins.

Perhaps we should take a clue from a winning strategy. Maybe other Believers would not feel that we are judging them if we are instead pointing them to Jesus and to his righteousness. *Ya think?*

The third audience that the Holy Spirit targets is the "prince of this world" and, by implication, his minions. And what does the Holy Spirit say to these evil forces? That they have lost the battle and are already judged and condemned by Jesus, the King of all Kings and Lord of Lords.

*"That power is like the working of his mighty strength, which he exerted in Christ when he raised him from the dead and seated him at his right hand in the heavenly realms, far above all rule and authority, power and dominion, and every title that can be given, not only in the present age but also in the one to come. And God placed all things under his feet and appointed him to be head over everything..."* [Ephesians 1:19-23, NIV]

We can listen to all sorts of sermons and seminars on the issue of spiritual warfare. We can hear many exhortations to bind Satan in this and bind Satan in that. But we see a clear pattern in what Scripture teaches us - all we need to do is to resist Satan, _remind_ Satan and his followers that they have already lost, already been defeated by an omnipotent God and his victorious Son. When we remind Satan that he has already lost the war, the Holy Spirit takes our words, combines them with what the Holy Spirit has already told Satan, and Satan is totally defeated at THAT VERY SECOND in whatever he is trying to do. But until reminded by us that he has already lost, Satan is the Ruler of this World and will continue successfully in whatever he is attempting to accomplish. Unless and until we remind Satan that he has already lost this war and choose to resist his lies, he will exercise power over us!

**Effective spiritual warfare is nothing more than reminding Satan of what is true, and the Holy Spirit is loosed to do the rest for us.**

Of course, a spiritually defeated or powerless life cannot utter effective spiritual claims. So we MUST be living like Jesus in the power of the Holy Spirit for any of our efforts at spiritual warfare to be effective.

And this just might call for us to encourage and exhort other Believers toward Christ. *Ya think?*

So what seems to be the Biblical teaching concerning ministering to others about the life, death, and resurrection of Jesus? What can we take away from John 16 where Jesus explains the ministry of the Holy Spirit after he is resurrected out of this world?

First, Christians should stop wasting time pointing out to unbelievers all their individual sins and transgressions, and instead point to their need for Jesus. This builds on what the Holy Spirit has already been doing, according to the words of Jesus.

Second, Christians should focus less on pointing out the individual weaknesses and sins of Believers (themselves and others), and instead focus on teaching and exhorting Believers (themselves and others) concerning the righteousness of Jesus. We need to show them the righteousness of Jesus by our lives and our words. This builds on what the Holy Spirit has already been doing, according to the words of Jesus.

Third, Christians can be less concerned about and not at all fearful of what Satan has done and is doing in this world, and simply stand firm on what we all know - Satan has lost the battle AND the war by the power of Jesus. When we stand on this truth, and remind Satan of it while we stand, then we will see victory over Satan EVERY TIME.

Please note that the entire range of activities by the Holy Spirit revolve around Jesus. Nothing that does not directly relate to Jesus is attempted by the Holy Spirit. Jesus is the beginning and the ending of every interaction involving the Holy Spirit and people, whether Believers or unbelievers. The issues may be quite different according to the target audience, but the message is the same: know Jesus, and then know Jesus better, and then live like Jesus is the King of Kings and you are adopted into his family as a victorious brother or sister!

Please note that the entire range of activities by the Holy Spirit revolve around Jesus. Nothing that does not directly relate to Jesus is attempted by the Holy Spirit. Jesus is the beginning and the ending of every interaction involving the Holy Spirit and people, whether believers or unbelievers. The issues may vary according to the target audience, but the message is the same: know Jesus, and then know Jesus better, and then live like Jesus is the King of Kings and you are adopted into his family as a brother or sister!


**Remember, the Holy Spirit's ministry is to:**
    **to show unbelievers their sinfulness**
    **to show believers Christ's righteousness**
    **to show Satan is defeat**

And as we follow these guidelines, as we point unbelievers and Believers alike to Jesus and his righteousness, few if any people will feel judged by you or me.

## Chapter Three

# DISCIPLESHIP AND THE GREAT COMMISSION

This ministry of developing and polishing Believers requires much from you and me. And it requires most of the tools God has given to his Church. This ministry can be accomplished from a pulpit, as in preaching; or in a classroom, as in teaching; or in your life, as in modeling the life and love and promises of Jesus to your family or friends. It can be accomplished in many ways, but perhaps the easiest to recognize would be the the one-on-one ministry which most people think of as discipleship. But we must realize that discipling involves all of the above, and more. For some insight, let's look at the *Great Commission* as stated in the 28th Chapter of Matthew.

> *"All authority in heaven and on earth has been given me. Therefore go and make disciples of all nations, baptizing them in the name of the Father and of the Son and of the Holy Spirit, and teaching them to obey everything I have commanded you."* [Matthew 28:18-20, NIV]

> *"All power is given unto me in heaven and in the earth. Go ye therefore and teach all nations, baptizing them in the name of the Father, and of the Son, and of the Holy Ghost; teaching them to observe all things whatsoever I have commanded you."* [Matthew 28:18-20, KJV]

The Greek word which is translated into the English word "go" is in the sense of "as you are going." In other words, the command here is not to go into all the world. The command is more like, "As you are going into all the world, make disciples."

A well-known Greek Interlinear Bible translates it this way: "Go, then, Disciple all nations..."

*The Great Commission did not demand that Believers preach the gospel. The Great Commission commanded that Believers make disciples!*

What Christians have for hundreds of years called the *Great Commission* was actually a command to make disciples throughout the world. While this does not mean that each and every Believer is commanded to be directly involved in a discipling relationship with at least one other Believer using a formal agenda, this DOES mean that the Body of Christ, the Church, should be continually involved in discipling Believers, teaching and training them to be sincere and mature Christians, and baptizing them into this new life with Christ.

A weekly alter call in your Sunday morning service does not fulfill Christ's command in the *Great Commission*. A regular visitation program by local church members does not fulfill Christ's command in the *Great Commission*. Sharing the Four Spiritual Laws with fellow students does not fulfill Christ's command in the *Great Commission*.

Actively discipling people fulfills Christ's command in the *Great Commission*.

> *"It was he who gave some to be apostles, some to be prophets, some to be evangelists, and some to be pastors and teachers, to prepare God's people for works of service, so that the Body of Christ may be built up until we all reach unity in the faith and in the knowledge of the Son of God and become mature, attaining to the whole measure of the fullness of Christ."* [Ephesians 4:11-13, NIV]

The purpose of the spiritual gifts that God hands out to Believers is quite simple: to teach, train and disciple other Believers until we are all Christ-like; until we are all mature and godly ambassadors for Christ; until we no longer need others' spiritual gifts.

The purpose of my gift of teaching is NOT for me to shoot off my mouth, but for me to teach and train and disciple others until they no longer need me to teach them. And then I get to start that process all over again with other Believers!

Let's take a closer look at *discipleship*: what it is, and how to do it.

A disciple, in my understanding, is one who is in a committed, submitted relationship where one Believer desires to learn and grow in his spiritual life in ways that require input from another Believer. I am not talking about the individual who decides that intense study and prayer is his preferred method of spiritual growth. While intense study of the Bible is an awesome pursuit, and the Holy Spirit may be the best teacher, discipleship goes further than this and *deeper* than this.

And I believe that the purpose of personal Bible study is to first help the Believer to know Christ better, and then for that Believer to help other Believers to know Christ better. The benefit is that BOTH of us learn more about God.

Individually, discipleship usually *starts* where one commits to a local church, a Body of Believers, where a preacher becomes one's primary spiritual leader and one learns from that pulpit leadership. Perhaps that Body includes Elders or other leadership positions, and maybe one or more of those other leaders has direct input into this one's spiritual development. But ultimately, discipleship almost always includes a situation where one Believer submits to another Believer and allows the other Believer's wisdom and insight to affect the first Believer's spiritual growth and development.

Whatever form this ministry of discipleship takes, discipleship's purpose is to develop my/your relationship with God in ways and to depths that would not occur if I/you relied exclusively on personally studying the Bible and asking the Holy Spirit for direction. After all, if AA can see the necessity of a "sponsor" then The Church should see the necessity of a discipler.

Please note that the entire gamut of activities by the Holy Spirit in this world revolve around Jesus. Nothing that does not directly relate to Jesus is accomplished by the Holy Spirit. Jesus is the beginning and the end of every action involving the Holy Spirit. The issues may vary according to the target audience, but the message to people is always the same: know Jesus, then know Jesus better, and then live like Jesus has already won every spiritual battle in your life!

*"When the Counselor comes, whom I will send to you from the Father, the Spirit of truth who goes out from the Father, he will testify about me.* [John 15:26, NIV]

*"When the Helper comes, whom I will send to you from the Father, that is the Spirit of truth who proceeds from the Father, He will testify about Me."* [John 15:26, NASB]

And I believe this is the purpose of all Spirit-led ministry to people on this earth: First, know Jesus; then, know Jesus better; and then to live like Jesus has already won every spiritual battle!

So how is this universal command to disciple other Believers, derived from the *Great Commission*, accomplished? Scripture gives many examples, options, and methods as to how Believers are to disciple other Believers.

*"Now there are diversities of gifts, but the same Spirit. And there are diversities of administrations, but the same Lord. And there are diversities of operations, but it is the same God which worketh all in all. But the manifestation of the Spirit is given to everyone to profit withal."* [I Corinthians 12:4-7, KJV]

*"There are different kinds of gifts, but the same Spirit. There are different kinds of service, but the same Lord. There are different kinds of working, but the same God works all of them in all men. Now to each one the manifestation of the Spirit is given for the common good."* [I Corinthians 12::4-7, NIV]

*Now there are varieties of gifts, but the same Spirit. And there are varieties of ministries, and the same Lord. There are varieties of effects, but the same God who works all things in all persons. But to each one is given the manifestation of the Spirit for the common good.* [I Corinthians 12:4-7, NASB]

This passage seems to say that God gives different gifts to different people as he deems necessary. And those gifts are manifested in different ministries, as he deems necessary. And those ministries are worked out, or managed, or performed or lived out, in different ways, as he deems necessary.

As an example, those with the gift of exhortation often end up in the pulpit of a church as preachers. But churches with an exhorting preacher may be run in different ways, or with different emphases or focuses. Or the exhorter could decide to establish a college campus ministry. Or the exhorter may just end up as a Sunday School teacher for junior high boys. There are many ways to manifest a gift, and many ways to run the ministry founded on that gift. But the ultimate result every Spirit-led ministry is that Believers end up looking and sounding and living more like Jesus.

And whatever the gift or the ministry, it is essential that God sets it apart and directs it as he chooses.

Our part, the part left to me and to you, is to follow Christ's lead and minister his Life to those God brings into our ministry. If we are open to God's leading, we will be discipling others, directly or indirectly, even if we are not aware of it. And if we are truly sensitive to God, and truly led by his Spirit, then we *will* be aware of it. In fact, we will be looking for it, wanting it, and reveling in it.

But often our words, or our efforts, result in different and sometimes unexpected responses from the people whose lives God allows us to touch.

Sometimes these different responses are a result of a little bit of flesh that enters our ministry efforts. Sometimes the flesh is on our part, and sometimes the flesh is on their part. But the flesh seems to manifest itself all too often.

However, I submit that most of the differences that we see in response to our attempts to minister and disciple is the result of the differences in the receptivity of the individual to whom we are ministering. Those who really want to grow in their spiritual life can't get enough spiritual input. Those who are not yet totally sold-out to God or have not grown to the place the Holy Spirit has wanted for that individual just don't grow as quickly, and sometimes just don't grow at all.

When we are looking for someone to disciple, to pour our hearts and lives into and watch them grow, to serve God as he commanded in what we often call the *Great Commission*, what type of individual should we look for and how should we minister to him or to her?

More specifically, do we want to teach the deep things of God to a person who may be a brand new Believer?

*"Brothers, I could not address you as spiritual but as worldly - mere infants in Christ. I gave you milk, not solid food, for you were not yet ready for it. Indeed, you are still not ready. You are still worldly."* [I Corinthians 3:1-2, NIV]

*"And I, brethren, could not speak unto you as unto spiritual, but as unto carnal, even as unto babes in Christ. I have fed you with milk, and not with meat: for hitherto ye were not able to bear it, neither are ye yet now able."* [I Corinthians 3:1-2, KJV]

Or, would we expect a strong spiritual walk from those who have not grown into the deep things of God; those who hear, who learn at least some, but do not grow?

*Of whom [Jesus] we have many things to say, and hard to be uttered, seeing ye are dull of hearing. For when the time ye ought to be teachers, ye have need that one teach you again which be the first principles of the oracles of God; and are become such as have need of milk, and not strong meat. For every one that useth milk is unskilled in the word of righteousness: for he is a babe.* [Hebrews 5:11-13, KJV]

*We have much to say about this, but it is hard to explain because you are slow to learn. In fact, though by this time you ought to be teachers, you need someone to teach you the elementary truths of God's word all over again. You need milk, not solid food! Anyone who lives on milk, still being an infant, is not acquainted with the teaching about righteousness.* [Hebrews 5:11-13, NIV]

I believe Scripture says that those of us who want to fulfill the *Great Commission*, who want to play a discipleship role in the lives of Believers, need to teach:

    1) the need to know Jesus to unbelievers;
    2) the basics of knowing Jesus to new Believers; and
    3) the riches of knowing Jesus to mature Believers.

BUT HOW CAN WE KNOW WHICH CATEGORY IN WHICH ANY PARTICULAR INDIVIDUAL BELONGS?

We must *judge* them. We must *evaluate* them. We must *assess* each person so as to fit our spiritual teachings to their current spiritual status.

And how do we judge them? We do not judge them strictly by their actions or attitudes because anyone can do the wrong things at any point in their spiritual lives. We judge them by their fruit because only Believers can produce good fruit. A quick assessment of someone's actions may lead to a wrong conclusion, but a quick assessment of their fruit will normally give a fairly accurate picture of the spiritual status of that individual.

*"You will know them by their fruits. Grapes are not gathered from thorn bushes nor figs from thistles, are*

*they? So every good tree bears good fruit, but the bad tree bears bad fruit. A good tree cannot produce bad fruit, nor can a bad tree produce good fruit."* [Matthew 7:16-18, NASB]

*"By their fruit you will recognize them. Do people pick grapes from thornbushes, or figs from thistles? Likewise every good tree bears good fruit, but a bad tree bears bad fruit. A good tree cannot bear bad fruit, and a bad tree cannot bear good fruit."* [Matthew 7:16-18, NIV]

Christians must become good fruit inspectors if they are to have an effective discipleship ministry with other people.

So if you want to be a good discipler, you must pick good people to disciple. They do not need to be mature Believers, wise in the things of God. But they do need to be good and faithful people.

*And the things you have heard me say in the presence of many witnesses entrust to reliable men who will be qualified to teach others also.* [II Timothy 2:2, NIV]

Paul himself gave us three different words to use when we refer to people, words that REQUIRE some degree of judgment on our part in order to use them accurately in our discipleship ministry. These words in the original Greek are:

1) *Gr-psuchikos* - natural man, unbeliever, does not know God
2) *Gr-pneumatikos* - renewed man, Believer, walking with God
3) *Gr-sarkikos* - carnal man, fleshly, a Believer no longer walking with God

To help us with recognizing the existence of these three groups of people, both Jesus and Paul gives us many descriptions of and prescriptions for each of these groups. And we are expected to use these descriptions, these tangible telltales, these spiritual measuring sticks, to qualify and quantify people into categories; _not_ to declare to ourselves or to others who is heading for heaven and who is heading for hell, but to _know better_ how to minister the things of God to someone with spiritual needs. And we are expected to use these prescriptions in our efforts to help others grow in their relationships with God.

And how can we know the spiritual receptivity and maturity of our potential disciples? We must learn how to Gr-_anakrino_ and Gr-_diakrino_, how to JUDGE other Believers.

Read on, dear Discipler...

## Chapter Four

# TIMING IN TRAINING

Let's say you are walking down a sidewalk in your city or town. And let's say that some driver runs a stoplight and hits another car. And let's say that car is pushed onto the sidewalk and strikes down a pedestrian. And let's say you are an off-duty paramedic who is also a strong Christian committed to Christ, and an Elder in your local church.

What do you do?

Do you rush over to the bleeding bystander and start quoting Scripture or ask him to pray the *"Sinner's Prayer"* with you so he can go to heaven if he died right then? Or do you immediately try to stop the bleeding and offer any other first aid you can?

Clearly, **society** would suggest that the most _urgent_ next step is to attempt any medical services you can to keep the bystander alive. But if you do that, you may never see this person again, and you would have missed your opportunity to assure that he might be ready to meet God in a meaningful way.

Clearly, **Scripture** would suggest that the most _important_ next step is to assure that the bystander is saved and in a righteous relationship with God. But if you do that, then the bystander may die before meeting God while being spiritually prepared.

In every decision and every action we take in this life, there is "a way to do things," an established or preferred or recommended or "wise" order in which we should act. And that order is totally dependent on the goals and objectives you hold for your life and the lives of those around you. In the above illustration, you have two choices, and these choices are totally dependent on the goals and objectives you hold for your life and the life of the person laying on the sidewalk in front of you.

This is the balancing act which the discipler must bear in mind all day every day. What are the goals and objectives for your Discipleship Ministry? And what are the goals and objectives you hold for the individual you are trying to disciple? And what do you use as the basis for establishing these goals and objectives?

There are so many motives and goals and objectives we can adopt in our walks with God and in our Discipleship Ministry. But we MUST align our motives and goals and objectives with the demands Jesus places on us through Scripture. Even a small error in our compass heading can result in missing our destination. This is inconvenient in our travels, but it can be disastrous in discipling.

One of the most common motivations in life is also one of the worst motivations for your Discipleship Ministry. This is the motivation to be happy or feel good, and to help your disciple to be happy or feel good. "If it feels good, it must be right" is a common slogan for this motivation. And this motivation can result in you doing or saying or teaching things inconsistent with Scripture, which would be counter to God's Plan for your Discipleship Ministry and for your disciple's life. And this motivation will totally destroy the sense of timing that the Holy Spirit wants to instill in your ministry. God gives us in Scripture many principles for our lives and our ministries, and he gives us great latitude and flexibility in implementing those principles. We can often justify using a hunch in how to implement Scriptural principles, but we must never substitute our hunches for the Scriptural principles themselves.

God doesn't want us to be happy – God wants us to be holy!

In our hedonistic world today, we hear all the time that God wants us to be happy. And many of us tend to see the Christian life in the same terms and with the same motives as the selfish and self-centered people around us. I still remember a Christian leader in Orlando, well-known in the area more than 30 years ago, telling me why he was in the process of divorcing his wife. He looked at me and too easily claimed that, "God wants us to be happy, and my wife just wasn't making me happy." His wife didn't make him happy any longer, and that was his motivation for violating his holy marriage covenant with her. Amazing!

Christian Hedonism controls the decisions and actions of too many Believers. So what controls the decisions and actions in your Discipleship Ministry?

*It is very important in discipleship that we always keep in mind the __FACT__ that God has a Plan for Christian growth and development, and that Plan requires that certain things are to be accomplished at certain times.*

In the very entertaining martial arts movie, *The Octagon*, the character played by Chuck Norris showed up late for a dinner date. After he apologized for his tardiness, the woman responded by saying, *"In my life, I have found that time means little. Timing, on the other hand, is everything."*

In my early attempts at discipling other men, I came face to face with this issue of timing as to certain issues or activities I felt needed to be addressed in the lives of the men I was discipling. One of my disciples had a problem with using profanity, and another one with using cigarettes. Both of these activities are usually seen by Christians as undesirable and even sinful activities. So I set about working with these men on their respective habits. And I saw great strides taken by those men. However, I also saw over time that some other spiritual issues were lacking in their lives, and these obvious shortcomings became very seriously manifest in their lives because I had focused these men on issues I had deemed important. The Holy Spirit revealed to me that because I had focused these men on certain issues that I had deemed spiritually important, the Holy Spirit was limited in what he wanted to accomplish in their lives. Had I been more sensitive to the Holy Spirit's timing, I saw in retrospect, I believe these men would have grown deeper and more powerful in their spiritual lives, resulting in the issues I had deemed important disappearing over time. My timing was imposed over top of the Holy Spirit's timing, and the men did not experience all the Holy Spirit wanted for them. It was my shortcoming and not their shortcomings that stunted their spiritual growth.

Apparently, timing is important to God. In fact, much of the ministry of Jesus here on earth was subject to a Plan and to a sense of timing in order to hold to that Plan. And part of that Plan involved in Jesus teaching the people by using parables.

Parables, as you know, are simple stories that have one clear application to the people listening to the story. Parables often don't have the same application to everyone in the world, so we must understand what the people listening to Jesus actually heard and what they "took home" from any given parable if we are to truly understand that parable.

**And Jesus told his disciples the very reason why he taught in parables: Jesus wanted people to learn things in a particular order and at a particular time.**

In fact, if you study the book of Mark verse by verse, you will see a pattern where early in the ministry of Jesus he told people to keep silent about what he had done for them. Jesus also required demons to keep silent about his identity. Jesus even taught truths that were _subtly_ contrary to Jewish views and traditions early in his ministry, and more _clearly_ contrary to Jewish views and traditions later in his ministry.

There was obviously a pattern of _progressive revelation_ in the ministry of Jesus, and he used parables as a teaching tool consistent with that pattern. And this progressive revelation applied to everyone listening to Jesus except, of course, when it came to his disciples. Jesus seemed to want his disciples to understand things more fully early on.

As a discipler, we must keep that pattern at the front of our minds. We must teach the basics to our disciples before we teach the deep things of God; we must feed them milk before we feed them meat; we must discern God's timing when we disciple others.

Sometimes this is because certain concepts will confuse the disciple, and sometimes it is because the concepts will cause the disciple to focus on something prematurely. But always it is so the disciple will learn the things of God in a proper sequence.

In the world of education, students learn basic biology and then advanced physiology before they learn surgery.

But I am getting ahead of myself...

It would seem that there is a timetable to God's dealing with people, and a timetable to their responses to his dealings.

For example, in the 4$^{th}$ Chapter of Mark, Jesus was teaching in parables again, and he stated that he did not want the people to fully understand what he was teaching at that point in time. And Jesus explained to his disciples why he was doing this.

> *When he was alone, the Twelve and the others around him asked him about the parables. He told them, "The secret of the kingdom of God has been given to you. But to those on the outside everything is said in parables so that, 'they may be ever seeing but never perceiving, and ever hearing but never understanding; otherwise they might turn and be forgiven!'"* [Mark 4:10-12, NIV]

The explanation Jesus gave to his disciples for why he taught the people in parables came directly from the prophet Isaiah in the *Old Testament*.

In fact, Jesus stated that he was teaching by parable "so that" the people would not understand fully at that time. Read Mark 4:12 again:

> *And He was saying to them, "To you has been given the mystery of the kingdom of God, but those who are outside get everything in parables, so that while seeing, they may see and not perceive, and while hearing, they may hear*

*and not understand, otherwise they might return and be forgiven."* [Mark 4:11-12, NASB]

*He told them, "The secret of the kingdom of God has been given to you. But to those on the outside everything is said in parables so that, 'they may be ever seeing but never perceiving, and ever hearing but never understanding; otherwise they might turn and be forgiven!'"* [Mark 4:11-12, NIV]

Here Jesus seems to be saying that the disciples *SHOULD* know the real meaning of the parable, but the others *SHOULD NOT* know the real meaning. At least not at that moment! The reference Jesus made was to the 6th chapter of Isaiah, where the prophet repents of not hearing and seeing God until the year King Uzziah died, and then Isaiah volunteers to take God's words to the people. And God says no because he didn't want the people to understand everything until certain things had occurred, otherwise they might respond prematurely. It might be the right response but it would be at the wrong time in their lives or the life of Israel.

In chapter six of Isaiah, God didn't want his words taken to the people until after certain events had been accomplished out of concern that they would respond prematurely. In Chapter Four of Mark, Jesus seemed to be saying something similar as his reason for speaking to the people in parables.

Yet he clearly wanted the disciples to understand.

*"And he said unto them, Know ye not this parable? And how then will ye know all parables?"* [Mark 4: 13, KJV]

Not only did Jesus expect them to understand this parable, but he seemed to say that understanding this parable was of paramount importance to understanding all the other parables he had taught so far and would be teaching in the future.

Jesus taught in parables so the people in general would not understand certain things prematurely and respond at the wrong time. Jesus practiced progressive revelation.

Jesus had a Plan for his ministry, and a timetable for what he taught. We must also have a Plan and a timetable in our Discipleship Ministry. And that Plan and timetable will probably be similar in general but different in details for each disciple.

You must take the time to pray often that God keeps you on track and within his timing as you seek to help others grow in their relationships with God. As you consider the vast array of materials available in this book and from others for use in your Discipleship Ministry, you must seek wisdom from the Holy Spirit as to how and when you implement those materials in the life of each disciple.

And how do you discern the timing necessary in the development and discipleship of each individual with which God gives you the privilege working?

You must learn the *Parable of the Soils*, and you must discern or judge the Soil Type of each disciple. It is the Soil Type that dictates the lion's share of the concepts and the timing of those concepts for that disciple.

## Chapter Five

# THE PARABLE OF THE SOILS

It is time we take a closer look at one of the most famous parables taught by Jesus. In this parable, we can see the different types of people, from fallen and close-minded people to excited and growing Christians, and we can also see the spiritual results of ministering into the lives of these disparate people.

Let's examine what many people call "*The Parable of the Seed*" or perhaps "*The Parable of the Sower.*" I truly believe this should be called "*The Parable of the Soils*" because the parable examines different types of soils. The Sower is the same, and sows the same Seed in all types of soil. The Seed is the same, and falls on all types of Soil. But the Soils each react or respond differently to the Seed. Consequently, Jesus was teaching about soils in this parable, and not sowers and not seeds.

The type of soil indicates the receptivity of the disciple.

Consider again that Jesus explained the seed as the Word of God. Jesus didn't claim that the seed was the Gospel. Jesus didn't say that sowing was sharing the claims of Christ. Jesus was talking about building into someone's life the Word of God, the whole counsel of God, the milk and the meat necessary to make strong and mature Believers.

***Jesus was speaking about the different types of soils.***

I believe this is the single most important parable that Jesus taught. And I believe this parable was intended to assist those who are called to minister to others in a discipling capacity.

What can we see about each of these soil types? We can see what stumbling blocks inhibit the growth of the Seed in each soil type, and what fruit comes as a result of each soil type. Proper understanding of this parable is _essential_ to the discipler who desires an effective discipleship ministry.

Jesus indicated the importance of this parable when he stated to his own disciples,

> _"Don't you understand this parable? How then will you understand any parable?"_ [Mark 4:13, NIV]

As far as we know, Jesus never said this about any other parable. He seemed to be declaring here that this parable was more important than any other parable for his disciples to understand. He seemed to be saying that his disciples have to understand this parable fully before they can understand any other parable. And Jesus linked the understanding of this parable with the "keys to the Kingdom of God" as he said,

> _"The secret of the kingdom of God has been given to you. But to those on the outside everything is said in parables..."_ [Mark 4:11, NIV]

**The disciples were given a special status in Christ's ministry, and were expected to have a complete understanding of certain things which the general population, even the typical Christian, was not expected to understand.**

Please read this parable once again, and we will examine it closely to see what God may have for us that we have never seen before. And then, after seeing, we will try to apply this parable to the call on Believers that Jesus proclaims in Matthew 28:18-20, which many call the _Great Commission_.

As we review this parable reported in Chapter Thirteen of Matthew, Chapter Four of Mark, and Chapter Eight of Luke, we see the same story but with a few additional details in one or the other Gospel account. For our purposes, we will look at Mark's perspective.

First, let's look at the context; what was happening shortly before Jesus taught this important parable.

Jesus had reached such popularity in his ministry that every place he stopped, he drew a crowd.  He would go to someone's house, and the people would crowd in around him with no apparent invitation.  He would walk down the street, and the street would be filled by the people following just to hear him speak.  Jesus could go no where without people hanging around and hanging on his every word.

So he began a pattern that became a sort of trademark for him: he would teach on the shore of the Sea of Galilee.  The Sea of Galilee, which was about 15 miles north to south and about 8 miles west to east, had high ground almost totally surrounding its northern edge.  Much of this high ground came close to the shore, making a steep slope down to the water's edge.  This steep slope created a natural amphitheater.  He would stand on the hillside just up from the shore and let the crowd gather below him, or he would sit in a boat just off-shore and let the people gather up the hillside on the shore.  Either way, up or down, the acoustics of the shore allowed his voice to travel farther and allowed him to reach more people.  Plus the outdoor setting allowed *more* people to come together from several nearby towns and villages.  With no local convention center available, this open theater was the best option available for speaking to large crowds.

So Jesus made arrangements to retain a boat for another off-shore teaching session.  Then he took his closest followers, *his disciples,* up the hillside for a private gathering.  There he formally appointed the twelve disciples from the dozens of men and women who were his closest followers.

Then Jesus and his disciples went into town for a meal at the house of a friend and supporter.  Naturally, the people followed him, invading the house and yard again without any apparent invitation.  There the people were crowding around Jesus and his disciples so closely that they couldn't even eat.  It seemed that no one wanted to miss anything Jesus said or taught.  Some teachers of the Law were in the crowd, and they were claiming that Jesus performed miracles through the power of Satan. Jesus responded with a teaching about the unpardonable sin.

While still surrounded by the crowd, Christ's family tried to get him to leave with them, apparently concerned that people would think that this simple carpenter from Galilee was nuts. Jesus took that opportunity to teach that anyone who follows God's will was his brother or sister or mother.

Then Jesus left the house (Scripture implies without his dinner but we don't really know) and went back to the Sea of Galilee to teach some more. As expected, the crowd from town followed him, and joined with the leftovers from the crowd that were still at the shore from earlier that day. So Jesus jumped into the boat he had previously arranged to be there, and pushed off a short distance from the shore. There, Jesus began to teach about a number of issues, including the *Parable of the Soils*.

When Jesus finished presenting this teaching session, he apparently took a break and wandered with his disciples through the crowd and up the hillside. When they finally got above the crowd where they could speak more freely, the disciples took the opportunity to ask Jesus why he taught in parables, and also about the meaning of this particular parable. Jesus explained to them that he taught the people in parables because they were not to know certain things just yet, but that the disciples were expected to know. He made two specific points to underline this explanation.

First, Jesus said, "*The secret of the Kingdom of God has been given to you,*" indicating his disciples, and not the people.

He went on and stated, *"But to those on the outside everything is said in parables so that..."* As I said before, this passage was a reference to the 6th Chapter of Isaiah. This *Old Testament* passage suggested that certain events must take place before the Jewish people of that time were supposed to fully understand certain issues. The implication here seemed to be that Jesus didn't want the general public to fully understand certain things at this point in his public ministry. Yet he wanted to teach them at least some of what he intended them to ultimately understand fully.

However, Jesus clearly expected his disciples to fully understand things, especially this particular parable. *"If you don't understand this one, how will you understand all the other parables?"* Apparently there was something about this parable that completed, that fleshed out, what Jesus wanted his disciples to understand about all the other parables he taught in order for the disciples to minister properly.

Then Jesus went into a detailed explanation of this parable for his disciples. But before we look closely at his explanation of the parable, let's first look at the general issue of sowing and farming as the Jews practiced it more than two thousand years ago.

As you would expect, farming back then was nothing like farming is today. Back then, a man would own a piece of property. Land at that time was used in pretty much only two ways: farming or herding. If a piece of land lent itself to farming, that is how the land was used. Otherwise, it was used for herding. The more steep or rough the terrain, the more obviously the land was destined for herding.

And farming included pretty much three separate functions: preparing, sowing, and then reaping. Preparing the soil entailed clearing everything off the land, and then plowing the dirt to loosen and break it up. There was no real fertilization; that was taken care of by crop rotation and leaving the soil to rest every few years. The *Old Testament* Law set down the principles for this. But it was necessary to uproot and remove any plants that got in the way of the crops. Weeds, other crops, rocks, and sometimes even trees, had to be removed before plowing and planting.

Once the soil was prepared, the sower would sling a bag of seed over his shoulder and walk all over the land throwing seed out at random. The bags were usually made of cloth or supple leather – Walmart hadn't started selling nylon backpacks yet. There was an attempt to cover the land evenly, but it was only an attempt. And the seeds lay on the ground until the rains came or the seeds sprouted into plants. When the plants matured and bore fruit, they were harvested by people walking all over the property picking or harvesting the crop.

Since the Sower walked all over the land sowing the seed, the land itself was weeded and tended by people walking all over the land during the growing season, and the crops were harvested by people walking all over the land. So there were paths in something of a pattern where the people could walk without stepping on the crops and destroying them. Every stalk of wheat and every ear of corn was precious to these people, just as they are to farmers all over the world today. So a pattern of pathways were used to walk the land without doing damage to the crops.

The Sower would walk all over the land using the pathways, and just throw the seed onto the plowed and prepared soil. But some seed would inevitably fall on or along the path itself. As you would expect, the soil on and along the path was packed hard from being walked on. When the soil is packed hard, the seed did not work itself into the dirt and sprout. This meant the seed along the path was exposed to the birds, which waited around during the planting season to enjoy the food being unintentionally served them by the farmer.

Obviously, the seed that fell onto the path was eaten by the birds long before it had the chance to sprout. This was the first type of soil in the parable.

Along the edges of a man's property close to his neighbor's land was often a narrow strip that was not cleared. This narrow strip of land was used to show the boundaries between properties. As such, the farmer seldom prepared this soil. It may be covered with rocks, weeds, thorn bushes, or even trees; anything that demonstrated the property line between one man's land and another man's land.

This rough and unprepared stretch of land constituted the next two types of soil in the parable.

And, of course, the fourth type of soil, the soil that was prepared and plowed, the vast majority of the man's land into which he poured so much of his effort and care, was the perfect soil for growing seed into great harvests.

Naturally, each and every person listening to Jesus that day knew and understood the importance of preparing soil before sewing the seed. Each and every person listening to Jesus that day knew the importance of using time and effort profitably, and knew to ignore or pretty much leave alone the first three types of soil. And each and every person listening to Jesus that day knew of the necessity of getting a good harvest from that fourth type of soil.

There are many possible lessons the typical Jew of 2,000 years ago could take away from this parable. There are only a few lessons that we can take away from this parable today. I submit that the single most important lesson we can all (all of us for the last 2,000 years!) take away from this is the importance of preparing the soil.

No amount of sowing can take the place of proper preparation of the soil first. It was soil preparation that was the most important process of this parable.

*It was soil preparation that dictated the response of the four types of soil!*

As we can see from the parable, even the Word of the Lord of Hosts cannot produce fruit if the soil is not properly prepared in advance.

From the *Parable of the Soils*, we can clearly see that the primary issue in discipleship is the type of soil. Any and all efforts at discipleship should be aimed at preparing the soil, and then continuing to develop that soil. With the soil properly prepared, the discipler need to do little in order to see much fruit.

Jesus almost tells us in this parable that if the soil is properly prepared, we just need to step back and watch the fruit come. Not quite, but almost. The bulk of the work of all discipleship occurred BEFORE the seed was sowed. And if we do the work of soil preparation properly, then the Kingdom of Heaven will see much fruit from our efforts.

In his absolutely awesome book, *"Principles of Spiritual Growth,"* Miles J. Stanford tells us that it takes a hundred years to grow an oak tree, and six weeks to grow a turnip. And it is obvious that the soil preparation for a turnip is totally different than for an oak tree. The people hearing Jesus that day knew all this.

**If we want to develop an oak tree that will last a hundred years, we need to put in more work and we need to prepare that soil much deeper.**

Over the forty-some years of my Christian life, I have heard *a lot* of people talk about "planting the seed." I have heard an argument with someone over what was and what was not sin described as "planting the seed." I have seen debates of religious issues that were totally lacking in love, where one of the participants later claimed, "Well, at least I planted the seed." I have witnessed Christians attempting to share the gospel, the message of salvation, with people who showed absolutely no interest in spiritual things, and later heard the Believer speak of the importance of sowing seed.

No matter how fruitless or how frustrating the response of the soil, that process of "sowing the seed" was portrayed as good and honorable, and ultimately productive.

But over these same forty-some years as a Christian, I have almost NEVER heard people speak of the importance of properly preparing the soil.

**If Christians were to spend more time, ANY time, preparing the soil around them, our churches would be full to overflowing every Sunday, and our homes would host Bible studies as often as we could make time.**

Proper preparation of the soil is difficult, time-consuming, challenging, and unbelievably fulfilling. It can be as simple as living a Christ-centered life in front of others, but usually involves more. Because soil preparation is so difficult and time-consuming, very few Believers take the time to perform this most important function.

But I am not sharing these concepts with you to encourage you to become a better farmer. I am sharing these concepts with you because I want you to become a better discipler.

And you become a better, a more effective, discipler if you can discern the type of soil you are working with in the Believer sitting before you. With that determination, you can help that Believer overcome the problems and spiritual obstacles that are common and predictable for that particular Soil Type.

Discipleship is the art of dealing effectively with the Soil Type of your disciple so he or she can grow properly, and then working with that soil to make it bear even greater fruit. If you know the Soil Type, Jesus gives the problems and their solutions right in the parable.

**In the Parable of the Soils, Jesus tells us exactly what is involved to work and improve that particular Soil Type!**

So, how do you discern the Soil Type of your disciple? How can you assess him or her without running the risk of violating Scripture's several commands to not judge?

You must learn how to judge other Believers, how to discern their spiritual level, through Scriptural measuring sticks, using spiritual rulers that allow you to measure the level of growth of the Believers in front of you.

**You must become <u>fruit inspectors</u>, able to examine and assess the spiritual fruit, listed in Galatians, which is manifest in the lives of those you want to disciple.**

*The acts of the sinful nature are obvious: sexual immorality, impurity and debauchery; idolatry and witchcraft; hatred, discord, jealousy, fits of rage, selfish ambition, dissensions, factions and envy; drunkenness, orgies, and the like. I warn you, as I did before, that those who live like this will not inherit the kingdom of God. But the fruit of the Spirit is love, joy, peace, patience, kindness, goodness, faithfulness, gentleness and self– control. Against such things there is no law.* [Galatians 5:19-23, NIV]

*Now the deeds of the flesh are evident, which are: immorality, impurity, sensuality, idolatry, sorcery, enmities, strife, jealousy, outbursts of anger, disputes, dissensions, factions, envying, drunkenness, carousing, and things like these, of which I forewarn you, just as I have forewarned you, that those who practice such things will not inherit the kingdom of God. But the fruit of the Spirit is love, joy, peace, patience, kindness, goodness, faithfulness, gentleness, self-control; against such things there is no law.* [Galatians 5:19-23, NASB]

As far as I have been able to discover, there are only two types of spiritual fruit discussed in the New Testament. And both are obvious to the fruit inspector.

The first type of fruit we can see in the lives of the man born blind in the 9th Chapter of John, and the Samaritan woman at Jacob's Well we have just seen described in the 4th Chapter of John. The blind man was healed and fell before Jesus and worshiped him. And the Samaritan woman went back to town and brought many people to see Jesus. These are natural responses in the changed lives that result from meeting Jesus. The sense of forgiveness and joy and freedom is almost impossible to contain, and usually results in grateful worship, and then gets spread around by the new Believer.

The second type of fruit can be found in Galatians, where Paul states: *"The fruit of the spirit is love, joy, peace, patience, kindness, goodness, faithfulness, gentleness, and self-control."* [Galatians 5:22-23, NIV] These inner attitudes are made manifest in the life of a new Believer as he or she allows God more and more control in his or her life. And these attitudes begin to affect pretty much every aspect of life in the new Believer, sometimes quite radically.

And if these fruit are not manifest in a Believer's life, it is a simple matter of discerning why. Pretty much the primary, and possibly the only, impediments to bearing fruit in a Believer's life are described in the *Parable of the Soils*.

Look at the *Parable of the Soils* again.

*Again Jesus began to teach by the lake. The crowd that gathered around him was so large that he got into a boat and sat in it out on the lake, while all the people were along the shore at the water's edge. He taught them many things by parables, and in his teaching said: "Listen! A farmer went out to sow his seed. As he was scattering the seed, some fell along the path, and the birds came and ate it up. Some fell on rocky places, where it did not have much soil. It sprang up quickly, because the soil was shallow. But when the sun came up, the plants were scorched, and they withered because they had no root. Other seed fell among thorns, which grew up and choked the plants, so that they did not bear grain. Still other seed fell on good soil. It came up, grew and produced a crop, multiplying thirty, sixty, or even a hundred times." Then Jesus said, "He who has ears to hear, let him hear." When he was alone, the Twelve and the others around him asked him about the parables. He told them, "The secret of the kingdom of God has been given to you. But to those on the outside everything is said in parables so that, "'they may be ever seeing but never perceiving, and ever hearing but never understanding; otherwise they might turn and be forgiven!'" Then Jesus said to them, "Don't you understand this parable? How then will you understand any parable? The farmer sows the word. Some people are like seed along the path, where the word is sown. As soon as they hear it, Satan comes and takes away the word that was sown in them. Others, like seed sown on rocky places, hear the word and at once receive it with joy. But since they have no root, they last only a short time. When trouble or persecution comes because of the word, they quickly fall away. Still others, like seed sown among thorns, hear the word; but the worries of this life, the deceitfulness of wealth and the desires for other things come in and choke the word, making it unfruitful. Others, like seed sown on good soil, hear the word, accept it, and produce a crop—thirty, sixty or even a hundred times what was sown."* [Mark 4:1-20, NIV]

It was only after saying to his disciples how important it was to have a full understanding of this parable that Jesus went on to give a full explanation of the parable. Jesus was saying things about this Parable that makes this Parable totally unique in all of Christ's teachings. Jesus explained in the *Parable of the Soils* just how people will respond to his love and his message. Jesus was teaching that all people will fall into one of four categories. And Jesus, right in his explanation of the Parable, revealed to his disciples just what to do with each of the categories.

He explains that the seed is the Word of God. Then he explains the four types of soil.

1. soil alongside the path that had been packed hard through frequent use. The soil was too hard for the seed to work its way into the soil and sprout. The Word was stolen by Satan before it could sprout or produce fruit.
2. soil that was never cleared and prepared, that had rocks and other things that restrict the seed from taking root and sprouting. This soil cannot support any real growth when exposed to pressures and persecution, and the plant withers.
3. soil that had possibly been prepared at least a little but still had thorn bushes and other similar impediments, and the seed takes root quickly and begins to grow. But the

growth is stunted, affected by many things, and it never grows into much of a plant nor does it produce any real fruit.

4. good soil that had been properly cleared, plowed, and prepared. The seed takes root, grows well, and produces much fruit.

These are the four types of soil that Jesus describes. And when it comes to your efforts at discipleship, these are the four types of people that you will be facing as possibilities for your ministry efforts. Look closely at the impediments to growth in each of them, and modify your ministry as necessary.

And we will take a closer look at each type of soil in the following chapters. Remember, Jesus used the teaching method here that he used often, that of a Parable. And we, each one of us who are a disciple of Jesus and who want to disciple others for Jesus, must remember that the soils in this Parable are PEOPLE! Soil is somewhat static, almost unchanging, and without feelings. People, on the other hand, change all the time, are blessed AND cursed with feelings, and are often totally unpredictable because of all that changing and all those feelings.

What I mean by this is quite simple – no matter how much you know about God, you have lots to learn about people. People are individuals, unique in almost every way. You invest time and energy into knowing and loving and serving God. THAT IS THE EASY PART! God explains himself in Scripture, and he remains unchanged throughout history. Individuals, however, change almost daily. There are more than 6 billion of them, and most of them try to remain inscrutable, hiding their deepest thoughts and feelings from you as long as they can.

*In many ways, it is easy to get to know an infinite and eternal God. In almost every way, it is difficult to know the individuals you are called to disciple.*

So you will have to remember that each one is different in some ways. What seems to work with some will not be as effective with others, and maybe not effective at all with still others.

In the *Parable of the Soils*, Jesus gave us a manual for discipleship, especially for what was needed to be done to make any specific disciple more fruitful.

So what does this manual of Christ's tell us about each type of soil? What does this manual tell us about discerning the type of soil represented in each of our disciples? What does this manual tell us about working each of the soil types to make them more fruitful?

This document cannot possibly be a complete discourse on the implications and the subtleties of discipling by Soil Type. But we can here BEGIN the discussion of discipling by Soil Types.

This book is an attempt to share with you some general guidelines and procedures that will help you be more effective in your Discipleship Ministry with most people. You, however, will have the hard part – discerning how to most effectively build into the life of each one you touch a deeper understanding of and stronger commitment to God.

## *Because that is what discipleship is all about – building another temple to love and serve and worship God.*

In the *Parable of the Soils*, we can clearly see that the primary issue in discipleship is soil preparation. Any and all efforts at discipleship should be aimed at preparing the soil, and then continuing to develop that soil. With the soil properly prepared, the discipler need to do little in order to see much fruit.

Jesus almost tells us in this parable that if the soil is properly prepared, we just need to step back and watch the fruit come. The bulk of the work of discipleship occurred BEFORE the seed was sowed. And if we do the work of soil preparation properly, then the Kingdom of Heaven will see much fruit from our efforts.

If we want to develop an oak tree that will last a hundred years, we need to put in more work and we need to prepare that soil much deeper.

# Chapter Six

# SOIL TYPE ONE

*The farmer sows the word. Some people are like seed along the path, where the word is sown. As soon as they hear it, Satan comes and takes away the word that was sown in them.*

The first thing a discipler of others MUST bear in mind is that no two people are alike. This means no two Soil Type One people are alike. We will discuss generalizations and averages and things that are typically true, but you must be the one to work through these ideas and concepts and come up with a detailed strategy to reach the person. No one can do it for you. And this will usually involve becoming a friend with the person.

The first Soil Type seems to have had no one to effectively work it and prepare it; or for our purposes, no one to disciple him or her. Also, please note that the soil is hard and unbroken through many people walking on it long *before* the seed fell on it. Also note that verse 3 says the seed fell – it was not sown. Any seed that falls on hard soil is an accident of sowing. Sometimes, this is what so many people refer to when they say, "I was just sowing the seed."

Please consider this - sowing seed to this soil is almost a total waste of time. The seed cannot sprout and it does not and cannot bear fruit. Satan is more in control of this type of person than God is.

But go back and look again: the soil was hardened BEFORE the seed was sown, and THEN Satan stole the seed.

The Soil Type One person has *chosen* hardness of heart. He or she has had the types of experiences that resulted in them withdrawing, retreating into themselves, believing that they and only they can care for themselves. Of the many Soil Type One people I have met, every one of them started out as Believers pursuing God, and they have had a difficult disappointment in their spiritual lives; some have had many disappointments. And they have become deeply wounded as a result. There is just too much pain or too much fear for the Soil Type One person to move forward in their faith. The Soil of their hearts has become hard from so many people and experiences trampling on that soil.

You or I will probably not know who those people or what those experiences were, but we will see early on in the relationship that Soil Type One has hardened soil for a heart.

And turning away from their initial views and beliefs about God is nothing more than a defense mechanism, a means to avoid confronting that hurt or fear from which they are hiding. It has become a natural and powerful reflex action to reject the things of God.

Sowing any seed into this type of soil is simply a waste of time. Clearly, the soil must be prepared before any seed can possibly take root. Soil Type One needs someone to prepare the soil before applying any seed.

**Soil Type One people need to be loved into a right relationship with God.**

It would seem that the last half of the first chapter of Romans speaks about this type of person. There, Paul tells us that God gave them over to a reprobate mind, allowing the person to plunge further and further from God and deeper and deeper into depravity. Regardless of what Paul was saying in Romans 1:18-32, here in the 4th Chapter of Mark Jesus is saying that this soil does not respond to the Word of God. And Jesus should know what he is talking about, right?

In Romans, Paul tells us:

*For the wrath of God is revealed from heaven against all ungodliness and unrighteousness of men who suppress the truth in unrighteousness, because that which is known about God is evident within them; for God made it evident to them. For since the creation of the world His invisible attributes, His eternal power and divine nature, have been clearly seen, being understood through what has been made, so that they are without excuse. For even though they knew God, they did not honor Him as God or give thanks, but they became futile in their speculations and their foolish heart was darkened. Professing to be wise, they became fools, and exchanged the glory of the incorruptible God for an image in the form of corruptible man and of birds and four-footed animals and crawling creatures.* [Romans 1:18-23, NIV]

This may not describe every Soil Type One person, but it describes many of them.

As I write this, I am listening to a conversation among several inmates of Federal Prison Camp - Pensacola. They have been discussing the many personal religious views of people around the world, and especially of one of the inmates, who described himself as an agnostic. The deeper issue being discussed revolved around the question, *"How can you know the Truth about God?"* After many minutes of discussion, this self-described agnostic claimed loudly, *"If I ever stand before the Creator and she is a Buddhist, and she asks me why I was not a Buddhist, I am going to tell her that she wasn't clear enough, that she didn't give us enough information to know. I am going to tell her that if she wanted all of us to know the TRUTH, she should have come down to earth and shown us the TRUTH."* Yes, he actually said this! He then paused as if looking for a response, so I didn't disappoint him. I called out, "God already did that 2,000 years ago." There was absolute silence for at least ten seconds, and then the man continued as if I had said nothing.

After 47 years of sharing the Living Word of God with Believers and unbelievers alike, I have never seen a hardened heart that wasn't hard by individual and personal choice.

***It is nothing to brag about when you continually sow seed onto this type of soil.***

*You don't sow seed into Soil Type One; you prepare the soil.* You work the soil. You break it up and till it and render it ready for seed. This soil MUST be softened or any seed you sow BEFORE you prepare the soil is going to be stolen by Satan.

In *Addendum A*, you can read an essay I wrote that accurately describes one particular manifestation of Soil Type One. Not everyone who would qualify as Soil Type One is described in *Addendum A*, but many of them are. Pay particular attention to the willful decisions, *the intentional choices*, that are described in the essay in *Addendum A*. When Satan claims a Soil Type One victim, they honestly believe their choices are a result of their own intelligence and reasoning power. They honestly believe that they have considered the issues and have come to the best conclusions possible under the circumstances. And they honestly believe they are right.

But they are wrong.

I won't say it is a waste of time trying to plant some seed. But Jesus himself described the Soil Type One individual as one where the Seed does not and cannot take root, does not and cannot sprout, and cannot grow into anything of spiritual value.

***Whatever you throw at Soil Type One, it is stolen away before it can take root or have an effect.***

Please understand this! Jesus did not claim they were a lost cause. I, myself have invested a lot of time and energy in Soil Type One individuals over the years. And I have found them all, or almost all, very interesting people. But they are convinced in their own minds that they know the truth, and that you and I are deluded into believing in some sort of myth. Many of them see us as deluded fools. Some of them see us as naive and gullible. But Soil Type One people see themselves as a higher intellect AT LEAST insofar as they have wisely avoided the trap of taking the Bible literally and seriously, and they see Believers in Christ as something less for not avoiding this trap.

These people will almost never respond to the Word of God in any sermon.  Remember that any and all Seed that is sown here is stolen before it can take root.   There is no possibility of rumination here – the Seed is stolen away before it can take root. They will not respond to the Word of God. But they just might respond to the Word of God _in YOU_! They won't accept Scripture verses but they just might accept the Scripture that you live out.  You must accept them and love them and **live** the Word of God in front of them.  It is only the Word of God _IN YOU_ that they will respond to and listen to and that they will ultimately accept.  They _probably_ won't, but they just might.  So if the Spirit of God leads you to minister to a Soil Type One person, this is how you get to them – through sharing your life over a long period of time.  According to what Jesus told us, merely preaching the Gospel will not and cannot get through to them.

You must understand this before going in.   Most Christians whom I have observed trying to minister to Soil Type One individuals have failed miserably.   And far too many of them have underscored the presumption of stupidity by saying stupid things.

Perhaps I need to relate to you my first experience with a Soil Type One individual.  Let me describe him.

He had a Doctor of Theology, a Th.D. so he could become a preacher and help people in a spiritual way.  Then he became a medical doctor, an M.D. so he could help people in a physical way.  Then he became an attorney, a J.D., so he could defend medical doctors in malpractice lawsuits.  He was a multi-millionaire because of his legal specialty.  And he was only 25 years old.

_THIS MAN WAS NOT STUPID!_

We talked for five hours.  I filled that time with all the evidence anyone could want as proof of God, Jesus, the Bible, and the man's need for salvation.  After five hours of names, dates, facts, and figures, this was his response to me.

*"Dave, you have done a great job, better than anyone else I have ever known. But still I won't believe that I needed Jesus to die for my sins, or that I am going to Hell because of not accepting it."*

He made everything quite clear. It was not a matter of evidence or logic or debate skills possessed by him or me. It was all a matter of his will, his choice.

Satan, along with his experiences, had blinded him.

And God used that experience to teach me that no one, no matter what evidence was presented, NO ONE could argue someone into the Kingdom of Heaven.

Remember this as you try to deal with Soil Type One.

Now go read the essay in *Addendum A*.

Oh, and one more thing to remember about the Soil Type One person: Satan is not in control of them. Satan has strong influence here, but he is not in control. No matter what happens in this person's life, we must remember that Satan requires cooperation from the Soil Type One person.

Satan may be the Master Deceiver, but the individual has made the choice.

And there is always the chance, even if microscopically small, that this person will opt out of Satan's Kingdom, stop believing the lies of Satan, and choose God. In my experience, Soil Type One people usually start out believing in Jesus and following his Word. But something happened early in his spiritual life that totally shook his faith and belief in Jesus. They were deeply wounded by discovering that there are intelligent people "out there" who believe in something similar, but different enough to bring down his faith. Doubt crept into his mind, and he began to listen to the lies of Satan. And he began to believe that his faith in Jesus was a lie.

So Soil Type One went looking for something he could believe in.

And he is still looking...

## *Your Strategy:*

Offer him something that he lacks, or that he has only in part – confidence. Confidence that you know God personally in a way that results in you knowing your eternal destiny. And confidence that he or she can know this, too.

## *His weaknesses:*

He believes that his intellect has saved him, or will save him, from any possible results of rejecting God. But he HAS to believe that, and he *knows* he HAS to believe that. He HAS to be in control of his future, so he HAS to believe in things that grant him control of his future. Consciously or unconsciously, Soil Type One HAS to be in control of his future so he HAS to believe in things that grant him control of his future. I can't stress this enough. Soil Type One people are totally driven by their need to be right and their doubt that they *are* right. So they never stop looking for the one clear truth. Not finding it, they will temporarily settle for several truths at the same time.

But they are always seeking the Truth!

They have no confidence in their eternal destiny, except in vague and usually undefined terms and concepts. Something like, "*Unite with the Universal Energy Pool*" or "*Unite with the Ultimate Cosmic Consciousness*" will usually be as concise as you will hear. Or they believe in reincarnation until they "*get it right*" according to some sort of eternal list of things to do "*right*" that has been demanded by some sort of undefined eternal being.

They usually believe that God cannot be known, but all of them believe that an increase in the knowledge of God will lead to a higher and more complete view of God.

They are unsure if heaven exists, or if they are going there; they are unsure if hell exists, or if they are going there.

They are almost certain to be unique in their views of God: they have their individual collection of choices from the Buffet Table of Eternal Beliefs, but they see that as a good thing. And they see faith in God and the Bible as a buffet item where they can pick and choose from this view and that view until they come up with their own composite picture of God. God is an invention of theirs, a result of what they and **only** they have taken from other beliefs and mixed together into one.

They have no desire to swim with the crowd in any way. They might even have a *fear* of being like anyone or everyone else.

Understand this and you will understand how NOT to deal with them.

And always remember that not even Jesus won every heart he wanted to win!

## *Assignments for Soil Type One:*

Soil Type One has only one impediment - hardness of the heart. That is a personal choice and may not be susceptible to any efforts on your part. Then again, it just may.

Working with a Soil Type One individual is a commitment to long-term change. You must take it slow. You are plowing and preparing the soil here, and that process may take a long time. So be prepared to invest many hours over many months. An alter call in one afternoon will never work with Soil Type One.

I would say to be prepared to think outside the box, but that would mean you are inside a box, exactly where you should NOT be. No one should be in a box until they die. But, anyway, be prepared to be unusual and unexpected. Soil Type One people believe that they are not part of the crowd, and maybe even above the crowd.

Early in your efforts to prepare the soil, you might try a Book Exchange. Let him or her pick a book or publication that best describes his or her views, and commit to reading it so you can understand those views better. But do so on the condition that he or she reads something you recommend for the same reason. If he or she does not agree to this exchange of knowledge, then you will get no where and you are wasting your time. If he or she agrees, then you can recommend the Gospel of John, or maybe *Mere Christianity* by C.S. Lewis, or maybe *Know What You Believe* or *Know Why You Believe* by Paul Little. Or choose another book or publication you have read and hope will appeal to the person. It would be best to use a book that majors in logic and reason rather than in Scripture. We have already seen that this person will allow the Word of God to sit there untouched until it is snatched away by Satan, so don't waste your time by quoting tons of Scripture or suggesting a book that quotes tons of Scripture. This person relies totally on their intellect, so appeal to their intellect.

Then discuss – not debate – his or her book. Then discuss – not debate – your book. Remember, you are dealing with someone who believes the intellect is most important, possibly of paramount importance, so your only way to make inroads into this person is to learn and discuss. Your effort here is an exchange of knowledge and not a debate. Besides, a Soil Type One person will almost always win a debate. And pray without ceasing that *"... God may grant them repentance leading to the knowledge of the truth, and they may come to their senses and escape from the snare of the Devil."* [II Timothy 2:25-26, NASB]

And never forget that Soil Type One people usually see all this God and heaven and eternity stuff as an intellectual exercise, not as a heart-felt faith. Your only hope is to let your heart-felt faith draw them.

You live it, and they will love it. It will almost certainly take a while. Or else they will go to hell. So pray for insight and wisdom and more faith, because sooner or later the Holy Spirit just may get through their egotistical barriers. Or maybe prompt you to move toward someone else.

Another strategy you can take to reach a Soil Type One person is to actually offer to discuss a Scripture passage, or even more than one Scripture passage. The problem here is the _guaranteed fact_ that the Soil Type One individual will not accept the accuracy, and especially not the spiritual authority, of the Bible. The individual will demand instead that you accept the spiritual authority of other writings by other religious leaders as equal to the Bible and to Jesus. The only response to this I have found to be a viable answer is to follow this line of reasoning:

> *"That just won't work. It isn't even an intellectually credible option, and you know it. If we accept the Bible, the Koran, the Bhagavad Gita and the writings of the Dali Llama as equal in spiritual authority, then we have to explain away or ignore the many places where they disagree with each other. Or else we have to delete the divergent sections of these writings. Because these*

*writings DO NOT agree except in generalities.  So what parts of the Bible do you want to throw out as unusable in order to accept the Bible as equally authoritative with the other writings?"*

Allow for an answer, which he or she will almost always want to avoid.  After any sort of answer, respond with something like:

*"I am sorry, but I cannot even begin a conversation with you under those conditions.  I cannot claim that the Bible has any spiritual authority and then ignore or cut out parts of that Bible.  The very <u>concept</u> of spiritual authority includes the presumption that this authority is above me.  I cannot presume that fact and, at the same time, claim that I have the authority to cut out any parts of what I have just admitted is an expression of God's authority.  And if you were intellectually honest, you cannot claim to have any authority above God's authority that allows you to cut out and ignore parts of what God claimed is his Word and what we have just established has spiritual authority.  We cannot claim that the Bible has spiritual authority and then arrogantly claim to have the authority to change the Bible."*

The only response to that which I have ever heard from this supposedly intellectual person is the claim that the Bible is a merely a collection of man's writings and has been subject to many translations and interpretations over the years.  As a result, certain (or ALL) sections are of suspect meaning.  And the only response to that proposition is:

*"If that is true, then you and I have to eliminate any real authority to the Bible.  We can't attribute to that book spiritual authority and, at the same time, claim that certain sections must be cut out.  Don't you see how intellectually hollow that proposition is?  Don't you see how foolish it is to claim that the Bible has any spiritual authority and still claim that we have the authority to disregard the parts we don't agree with?"*

Do you see where we are going with this line of reasoning?  The Soil Type One person wants to grant at least some spiritual authority to the Bible for purposes of discussion, but at the same time, absolutely MUST reserve the right to edit the Bible so it fits his beliefs.  And he or she KNOWS how stupid that line of reasoning really is.

Now go and read the essay in Addendum A.

---

Remember, you MUST understand that the Soil Type One individual considers his or her intellect to be the authority on all things religious, and yet cannot admit to that presumption.  He or she simply cannot consciously claim to be that arrogant!  But they still believe it deep down inside.

## Chapter Seven

# SOIL TYPE TWO

*Others, like seed sown on rocky places, hear the word and at once receive it with joy. But since they have no root, they last only a short time. When trouble or persecution comes because of the word, they quickly fall away.*

The second type of soil does not allow any roots, because it was never properly cleared and prepared. It was still full of rocks and other things that get in the way of the seed properly growing. As a result of the rocky soil, the roots cannot grow. Because of poor roots, others see puny plants and no fruit. They laugh and make fun of what is growing there, subjecting it to ridicule and persecution. The plants can't take the "heat" of that ridicule and persecution and they just shrivel up.

Specifically, this person accepts Christ in a meaningful way and is truly excited by the feelings of freedom from guilt and joy in the Holy Spirit. Every day is more exciting than the day before, and every day brings happiness in new and different ways. And then, suddenly, without warning, reality jumps up and bites them. The happiness is blown away, even if for only a few minutes.

Please note: this is not a problem with Satan stealing their joy. This is a problem of spiritual immaturity resulting from shallow spiritual roots.

Simple things like spiritual weakness or even spiritual setbacks become the enemy for Soil Type Two people. Because they accepted God's truth on primarily an emotional level, they tend to pursue those Scriptures which result in them feeling good about following Jesus. They memorize passages that emphasize love and happiness and security, like *"Beloved, we know that we are sons of God, and if sons, then we are joint-heirs with Christ."* They sing songs that claim *"Jesus is the answer,"* and *"Every day with Jesus is sweeter than the day before,"* as if there is nothing else of any importance in all the universe than feeling good about following Jesus. Soil Type Two people love the idea of being a "King's Kid" because it makes them feel important and loved and accepted. And they <u>really</u> love the benefits that some spiritual leaders wrongly teach is deserved by and owed to "King's Kids." Specifically, many of these leaders teach that all you have to do is claim it, and God will give it to his children. Not only does this wrong teaching appeal to a Soil Type Two's insecurities, this teaching also appeals to his or her greed and selfishness. So the Soil Type Two person often finds that any teaching which makes them feel warm and good and happy and, of course, wealthy is a teaching he or she can embrace.

> *For the time will come when they will not endure sound doctrine; but wanting to have their ears tickled, they will accumulate for themselves teachers in accordance to their own desires, and will turn away their ears from the truth and will turn aside to myths.* [II Timothy 4:3-4, NASB]

These people tend to believe deep down inside that the most important result of knowing and following Christ is the fact that they are happy. Some of them use words and phrases and verses that make it sound almost like they are having a love affair with Jesus.

In fact, any teaching that appeals to a shallow walk with God will find an open heart from a Soil Type Two person. And it is the job of the discipler to assist these people to get rooted and grounded in God's Living Word so they become more like Jesus, who never claimed material goods in his Father's Name.

Since Soil Type Two people tend to focus on Scriptures that make them feel good, they are often made uncomfortable by passages like:

*But in whatever respect anyone else is bold—I speak in foolishness—I am just as bold myself. Are they Hebrews? So am I. Are they Israelites? So am I. Are they descendants of Abraham? So am I. Are they servants of Christ?—I speak as if insane—I more so; in far more labors, in far more imprisonments, beaten times without number, often in danger of death. Five times I received from the Jews thirty-nine lashes. Three times I was beaten with rods, once I was stoned, three times I was shipwrecked, a night and a day I have spent in the deep. I have been on frequent journeys, in dangers from rivers, dangers from robbers, dangers from my countrymen, dangers from the Gentiles, dangers in the city, dangers in the wilderness, dangers on the sea, dangers among false brethren; I have been in labor and hardship, through many sleepless nights, in hunger and thirst, often without food, in cold and exposure. Apart from such external things, there is the daily pressure on me of concern for all the churches. Who is weak without my being weak? Who is led into sin without my intense concern? If I have to boast, I will boast of what pertains to my weakness. The God and Father of the Lord Jesus, He who is blessed forever, knows that I am not lying. In Damascus the ethnarch under Aretas the king was guarding the city of the Damascenes in order to seize me, and I was let down in a basket through a window in the wall, and so escaped his hands.* [II Corinthians 11:23-33, KJV]

It is unfortunate, but Soil Type Two people love the good parts but fear the bad parts of Scripture. Not on a conscious level, usually, but on an unconscious level that affects their day-to-day lives. They often live by the unstated belief that following God makes them happy, and that very happiness subtly becomes their reason for following God.

So Soil Type Two people often look for "signs" that God approves of them. They tend to latch onto the concept of laying out a fleece, as we see in the book of Judges. There the tribe of the Midians continually killed the crops and livestock of the Hebrew people. So God approached Gideon and made him a promise.

> *The LORD turned to him and said, "Go in the strength you have and save Israel out of Midian's hand. Am I not sending you?"* [Judges 6:14, NIV]

After hearing this, Gideon called a bunch of Israelites together to announce his plans for battle. And Gideon wanted a sign that God was truly going to accomplished what he promised to do.

Gideon's fleece was not a sign of faith, nor is it a sign of faith when the Soil Type Two person follows his example. It is a sign of weakness, of not believing what God has told you or shown you. It is asking God to *"prove it after he has promised it."*

A Soil Type Two person uses Gideon's fleece approach to gain additional assurance and hope and that God will live up to his words. The Soil Type Two person needs a constant assurance that God loves them and will do what he promises. This is why they love to dwell on the Scriptures and the songs that offer these assurances. The Soil Type Two person usually needs to keep their emotions high in order to keep following God.

In many ways, these people often resemble the stereotypical "groupie" that follows rock stars and famous actors and important politicians around. They long for and demand the feelings of excitement that result from feeling a part of something important. And don't forget that ALL groupies are sincere. Soil Type Two people do not put on an act! They do not put on a show. Soil Type Two people are not fake followers of Christ!

But since they need constant hope and assurances that God loves them and accepts them, they are susceptible to losing that assurance when they do something wrong; when, without warning, they slip up and do or say something that does not properly represent the person and nature of Jesus. Something as simple as stubbing their toe and swearing about it can set back their feelings for God, and therefore their walks with God. Maybe they felt guilty, or maybe they felt condemned by God. But they no longer felt happy. They remembered that in Christ they are supposedly a new creature, and that all things have become new, yet this was clearly a reaction from the past when they did not know God. Even worse, maybe their ungodly reaction was acted out in front of someone who then was critical of that reaction.

Maybe someone saw them manifest their humanness and made fun of them or called them a hypocrite. Maybe it was their own thoughts that condemned them. Whatever happened, they felt like a spiritual failure. They felt like they had failed God. The more this "failure" happens, the stronger their feelings of failure. And sooner or later, they just give up trying to follow Jesus. Striving to follow God no longer made them happy, and that fact combined with other negative feelings result in them turning their back on their faith in Jesus. It may not be a conscious decision, but it was a decision.

Remember, Jesus pointed out that their problem was spiritual in nature. It was "*trouble or persecution comes because of the Word*" that resulted in them falling away.

The Soil Type Two person is spiritually weak because he or she bases their spirituality on how they feel, and NOT on the *FACT* that Jesus has saved them and transformed them into an eternal being. They may have "feet of clay" but they are definitely a child of God. Yet they don't *feel* like a child of God, and their feelings tell them they are NOT a child of God. It is their feelings and not the Word of God that controls their day-to-day spiritual life. And their feelings tell them that their salvation just didn't work.

A spiritual roller coaster is difficult for anyone to deal with. It is especially difficult for someone whose emotions are in control of them to deal with. For a Soil Type Two person, spiritual depression creeps in entirely too easily. They become incapable of standing firm in the power of the Holy Spirit, and sooner or later they fall away. This is a cycle with the Soil Type Two person, a cycle repeated often unless someone takes the time and effort to help them grow beyond their soil type.

Paul's prayer for the saints at Ephesus comes to mind here, and it would be a good prayer for all disciplers to remember:

*But because of his great love for us, God, who is rich in mercy, made us alive with Christ even when we were dead in transgressions—it is by grace you have been saved. And God raised us up with Christ and seated us with him in the heavenly realms in Christ Jesus, in order that in the coming ages he might show the incomparable riches of his grace, expressed in his kindness to us in Christ Jesus. For it is by grace you have been saved, through faith—and this not from yourselves, it is the gift of God — not by works, so that no one can boast. For we are God's workmanship, created in Christ Jesus to do good works, which God prepared in advance for us to do.*

*For this reason I kneel before the Father, from whom his whole family in heaven and on earth derives its name. I pray that out of his glorious riches he may strengthen you with power through his Spirit in your inner being, so that Christ may dwell in your hearts through faith. And I pray that you, being rooted and established in love, may have power, together with all the saints, to grasp how wide and long and high and deep is the love of Christ, and to know this love that surpasses knowledge—that you may be filled to the measure of all the fullness of God.* [Ephesians 2:4-10, and 3:14-19, NIV]

*For more insight on the emotional processes of a Soil Type Two person, you can read an essay I have written about these people in Addendum B.*

As usual, this essay does not describe all Soil Type Two people, and it may describe people who are NOT Soil Type Two people.  But the need for spiritual approval and spiritual demonstrations is a common weakness for Soil Type Two people.  Read the essay in _Addendum B_ to understand most of these people better.

# Your Strategy:

You must help them count on and believe that it is the Word of God which dictates all reality, that it is the Son of God who loves them and forgives them, and that it is the Spirit of God who will help them grow beyond any and all problems.

You must help them grow to the point that they can suppress their feelings concerning their standing before God when they feel that their Heavenly Father has abandoned them because of some thought or action on their part, and instead rely on the promises of God as recorded in His Word.

*You must help them realize that their perceptions are nothing but theories about reality!*

Review the following verses.   Learn them yourself; hopefully memorize them; preferably memorize them _with_ your disciple.  Look for practical lessons in life that relate to one or more of these verses, and share those lessons with him or her. To apply these verses, and the spiritual lessons learned from these verses, is the only way for Soil Type Two people to grow out of spiritual immaturity into spiritual maturity.

# Their weaknesses:

These people let their circumstances control their lives in Christ, rather than the Spirit of God.  And their circumstances are strongly influenced by their feelings.  They allow their feelings to indicate how close they are to God at any given moment.  They believe that when their feelings are not so warm and wonderful towards God, that they are somehow not close to God anymore.  They seek out spiritual experiences that make them feel good or feel happy, and they see these experiences as indicators that their life in Christ is working and profitable and Scriptural.

They tend to have devotions instead of Bible study, where they can get assurances of God's love for them and feel good about those assurances. They tend to major on *feeling* loved and accepted by God, which they see as actually *KNOWING* God.

These people suffer a spiritual roller coaster life, sometimes on a daily basis. And they live for the spiritual high.

Remember, with a Soil Type Two person, it is usually not a conscious choice to fall back into sin; it is usually a matter of not feeling the love for Christ that he or she once felt, which leads to spiritual depression, and ultimately to giving up. They need to review the following verse frequently:

*Yet I hold this against you: You have forsaken your first love. Remember the height from which you have fallen! Repent and do the things you did at first.* [Revelation 2:4-5, NIV]

*Nay, in all these things we are more than conquerors through him that loved us. For I am persuaded, that neither death, nor life, nor angels, nor principalities, nor powers, nor things present, nor things to come, nor height, nor depth, nor any other creature, shall be able to separate us from the love of God, which is in Christ Jesus our Lord.* [Romans 8:37-39, KJV]

*We live by faith, not by sight.* [II Corinthians 5:7, NIV]

# Assignments for Soil Type Two:

These people need your help to take the focus and the emphasis *off* their feelings and place it *on* the Word of God. If the Word of God says it, it must be true.

Help them, don't tell them, to memorize a few Scriptures that deal with their assurance of Salvation. Passages like the following:

Taken from *The Handbook of Bible Application*, Neil S. Wilson, Editor, Tyndale House Publishers:

BIBLE READING: Exodus 13:17-22
KEY BIBLE VERSE: *By day the Lord went ahead of them in a pillar of cloud to guide them on their way and by night in a pillar of fire to give them light, so that they could travel by day or night.* (Exodus 13:21, NIV)
**Firm assurance is based on God's Word.** God gave the Hebrews a pillar of cloud and a pillar of fire so they would know day and night that God was with them on their journey to the promised land. What has he given us so that we can have the same assurance? The Bible—something the Israelites did not have. Look to God's Word for reassurance of his presence. As the Hebrews looked to the pillars of cloud and fire, we can look to God's Word day and night to know he is with us, helping us on our journey.

BIBLE READING: Luke 21:5-19
KEY BIBLE VERSE: *Make up your mind not to worry beforehand how you will defend yourselves.* (Luke 21:14, NIV)
**Firm assurance is based on God's care for us.** Jesus warned his followers of coming persecutions in which they would be betrayed by their family members and friends. Christians of

every age have had to face this possibility. It is reassuring to know that even when we feel completely abandoned, the Holy Spirit stays with us. He will comfort us, protect us, and give us the words we need. This assurance can give us the courage and hope to stand firm for Christ no matter how difficult the situation

## And other passages, like:

*And ye shall be hated of all men for my name's sake: but he that endureth to the end shall be saved.* [Matthew 10:22, KJV]

*As a result of this many of His disciples withdrew and were not walking with Him anymore. So Jesus said to the twelve, "You do not want to go away also, do you?" Simon Peter answered Him, "Lord, to whom shall we go? You have words of eternal life. We have believed and have come to know that You are the Holy One of God."*
[John 6:66-69, NASB]

*And when they had preached the gospel to that city, and had taught many, they returned again to Lystra, and to Iconium, and Antioch, confirming the souls of the disciples, and exhorting them to continue in the faith, and that we must through much tribulation enter into the kingdom of God.* [Acts 14:21-22, KJV]

*And we know that in all things God works for the good of those who love him, who have been called according to his purpose.* [Romans 8:28, NIV]

*No, in all these things we are more than conquerors through him who loved us. For I am convinced that neither death nor life, neither angels nor demons, neither the present nor the future, nor any powers, neither height nor depth, nor anything else in all creation, will be able to separate us from the love of God that is in Christ Jesus our Lord.* [Romans 8:37, NIV]

*Therefore, my beloved brethren, be ye stedfast, unmovable, always abounding in the work of the Lord, forasmuch as ye know that your labour is not in vain in the Lord.* [1 Corinthians 15:58, KJV]

*Be on the alert, stand firm in the faith, act like men, be strong.* [1 Corinthians 16:13, NASB]

*And he died for all, that those who live should no longer live for themselves but for him who died for them and was raised again.* [2 Corinthians 5:15, KJV]

*Therefore, my brethren dearly beloved and longed for, my joy and crown, so stand fast in the Lord, my dearly beloved.* [Philippians 4:1, KJV]

*Therefore, brethren, stand fast, and hold the traditions which ye have been taught, whether by word, or our epistle. Now our Lord Jesus Christ himself, and God, even our Father, which hath loved us, and hath given us everlasting consolation and good hope through grace, comfort your hearts, and establish you in every good word and work.* [II Thessalonians 2:15-17, KJV]

*I know your afflictions and your poverty—yet you are rich! I know the slander of those who say they are Jews and are not, but are a synagogue of Satan. Do not be afraid of what you are about to suffer. I tell you, the devil will put some of you in prison to test you, and you will suffer persecution for ten days. Be faithful, even to the point of death, and I will give you the crown of life. He who has an ear, let him hear what the Spirit says to the churches. He who overcomes will not be hurt at all by the second death.* [Revelation 2:9-11, NIV]

Now read the essay in Addendum 2.

And we must never forget the words of Jesus, when he told us:

*These things I have spoken unto you, that in me ye might have peace. In the world ye shall have tribulation: but be of good cheer; I have overcome the world.* [John 16:33, KJV]

## Chapter Eight

# SOIL TYPE THREE

*Still others, like seed sown among thorns, hear the word;
but the worries of this life, the deceitfulness of wealth and
the desires for other things come in and choke the word,
making it unfruitful.*

This third type of soil apparently received at least some work, but the job wasn't done well or else it was not complete. Thistles, weeds, and other impediments get in the way of the plants growing, stunting any growth and development of the plants. The plants may grow at first, but they never grow to maturity and never show signs of any real fruit because other things (thorns) are competing for the limited nutrition and attention.

Soil Type Three is even more common than Soil Type Two. In fact, it seems sad but it often looks like Soil Type Three is the norm in most churches around the world. These people hear the Word and respond to it. But they are spiritually shallow and immature, and they allow the *"cares of this world, and the deceitfulness of riches, and the lusts of other things"* to get in the way of their walks with God. They will have a constant "up and down" experience with the Creator of the Universe. The result, again, is shallow and immature plants producing little or no fruit.

The third Soil Type is easily distracted from the things of God, and must receive some constant instruction and training on personal discipline and focus in order to remain a viable plant and to, ultimately, bear fruit. Daily contact with them is important, especially to share what you learn from your personal quiet time with God, and ask what they have learned from theirs. Let them see you successfully apply what you learn to your life. They need to see Biblical and spiritual solutions to life's questions and problems so they are not so concerned with how the world handles things.

Soil Type Three people have a heart for God, but they let their circumstances get in the way of their spiritual growth. Maybe it is academic studies, maybe it is participation in sports, maybe it is a job or taking care of the home and the children; whatever it is, Soil Type Three people allow activities and concerns to take their eyes off of the important issues and put them instead on the urgent issues.

Years ago, back in college when I was a fairly new Christian, I was having the same problem. I had a full load of classes, I was leading two Bible Studies each week with four or five students each, and I was one of the student leaders in a large campus ministry. This meant that I had a third weekly Bible study to attend, a weekly leadership meeting to attend, weekly student meetings that I had to prepare for, and a weekly meeting with the campus director of that ministry. In addition, I had a leadership position in a small church just off campus where I led the high school Sunday School class along with a Wednesday night adult Bible study. I was so busy reaching out to and ministering to others, along with being ministered to myself by others, that I was totally missing out on allowing God to minister to me. I was studying the Bible to increase my knowledge of God [*Gr-gnosis*] for the ministry activities I was involved in, but I was not looking to the Word of God to know him better [*Gr-epignosis*]. I needed to change my perspective and my priorities. A fellow college student gave me a copy of a booklet called *"Tyranny of the Urgent."* This booklet illustrated these problems in a way that was very meaningful to me. I have no idea who the author was, nor if this booklet is still available, but it was of monumental importance to my spiritual growth.

The entire premise of the book was that many of us allow the *urgent* things (the issues that seem so important to us as we examine and schedule our day, the issues which have a clear time constraint) to crowd out the *necessary* things (the things essential to our spiritual growth, the activities required for our walks with God to increase).  Why?

*Because the urgent issues have a real time constraint, and the necessary issues don't. Urgent things place a clear demand on our lives and necessary things don't.*

Soil Type Three people tend to let their spiritual lives slide as they get involved with the things that life throws at them. Sometimes these things are a result of personal choices, like the Bible studies that I led and participated in.  Sometimes these things are simply the result of living, like school and jobs and family.  But ALWAYS these things take enough time that they don't allow time spent with God just getting to know him better.

As a result, personal spiritual growth takes a back seat to life's activities and concerns.  This is the Soil Type Three that Jesus was referring to.

In *Addendum C*, you will find an essay I wrote that addresses one of the reasons the Soil Type Three person seems too busy and over-committed, and it gives insight on how to focus these people.  Reading it will help you help them to get their priorities right and pursue the freedom and joy God desires for them in this life.

# Your Strategy:

These people have primarily two different but related problems, and any discipleship strategy absolutely must include a prescription for both of them. The first problem is faith, or a lack thereof. The second is discipline, without which all sorts of issues in life will always creep into dominance in these people's lives. When we continually place our faith in God, we can KNOW that his Son, Jesus, will always walk at our side, and the Holy Spirit will always guide our lives. And when we add some discipline to that, we can know that we will perform as expected.

*So faith comes from hearing, and hearing by the word of Christ.* [Romans 10:17, NASB]

With faith in God, he will DIRECT our steps. With a little discipline added, we know that we will TAKE those steps.

Remember that Soil Type Three people actually try hard, perhaps too hard, to please God. But they also try hard to accomplish too many other goals and objectives. It is simply not possible to accomplish everything in life that these people feel compelled to accomplish. Life for them really is a problem of priorities.

# Their weaknesses:

These people mean well but seem to be disorganized and easily disillusioned. They know what to do but feel like they seldom do it. They want to walk down the right path but seem to stray on a regular basis. They can talk the talk quite well, but they are often surprised, even amazed, at how regularly they do not walk the walk. Without realizing it, their spiritual instability is often a result of fear – they fear NOT doing the _right_ things in life so they try to do _everything_ in life. And trying to do everything in life results in some things just not getting done.

*For I testify about them that they have a zeal for God, but not in accordance with knowledge.* [Romans 10:2, NASB]

The urgent things in life are standing up and demanding attention, so these people have little problem with doing the urgent things in life, the things that demand their attention. But the things which are usually _not_ done are the necessary things in life.

They clearly see their inability to find the time to do the right things, so without realizing it they tend to pursue riches in many things and in many ways so they can then afford the time to do the right things. And they pursue achievements because that usually produces money. Riches, and the concerns that always follow riches, slowly and subtly becomes the goal, but they usually pursue riches with the same disorganized efforts that they pursue God. The result is often very little accomplishment in anything the person pursues in life, especially spiritual accomplishments. So they get discouraged and even depressed, and sooner or later just stop trying very hard. They keep up appearances, but nothing more. They usually keep going to church and they may even attend weekend seminars and Christian music concerts. But what often seems like a wonderful Christian life is hollow and empty. Something just doesn't seem right, not to them and not to others.

These people need your help to focus on the necessary things, then prioritize the urgent things, and then *Just Do IT!*

I have written an article that applies to many people who call into th Soil Type Three category. If this article applies to your disciple, then it will help you to better understand and better minister to your disciple.

You can find this article in Addendum C.

# Assignments for Soil Type Three:

The Apostle Paul was great at using sports phrases and analogies to communicate the importance of staying the course, of doing what is necessary.  You should consider using some of Paul's words to encourage and focus and motivate these people.  Scripture memory is always valuable, but it is more important that you talk through these passages with them, making sure they actually _understand_ the things Paul was saying.  With these people, it is often enough that they _understand_ what is necessary, and then they will _do_ what is necessary.  But you must keep up with them, stay on top of things, and use any sports phrase you need in order to motivate you to stay involved.  These people need to see you do it right, and need your encouragement that they can do it right.  But most of all, these people need your time and your commitment and your love. They need to see and know that you will love them and stand by them no matter how many times they fail.  This, more than anything else, will keep them from giving up.  And giving up is always the ultimate failure in sports _AND_ faith.

Review the following verses with them.  Learn them yourself; hopefully memorize them; preferably memorize them _with_ your disciple.  Look for practical lessons in life that relate to one or more of these verses, and share those lessons with him or her.  To apply these verses, and the spiritual lessons learned from these verses, is the only way for Soil Type Three to grow out of spiritual immaturity into spiritual maturity.

Perhaps the most important Scripture for Soil Type Three to learn and apply, and preferably _memorize_, would be:

> _Therefore, since we are surrounded by such a great cloud of witnesses, let us throw off everything that hinders and the sin that so easily entangles, and let us run with perseverance the race marked out for us. Let us fix our eyes on Jesus, the author and perfecter of our faith, who for the joy set before him endured the cross, scorning its shame, and sat down at the right hand of the throne of_

*God. Consider him who endured such opposition from
sinful men, so that you will not grow weary and lose heart.
In your struggle against sin, you have not yet resisted to
the point of shedding your blood. And you have forgotten
that word of encouragement that addresses you as sons:
"My son, do not make light of the Lord's discipline, and
do not lose heart when he rebukes you, because the Lord
disciplines those he loves, and he punishes everyone he
accepts as a son." Endure hardship as discipline; God is
treating you as sons. For what son is not disciplined by
his father? If you are not disciplined (and everyone
undergoes discipline), then you are illegitimate children
and not true sons. Moreover, we have all had human
fathers who disciplined us and we respected them for it.
How much more should we submit to the Father of our
spirits and live! Our fathers disciplined us for a little
while as they thought best; but God disciplines us for our
good, that we may share in his holiness. No discipline
seems pleasant at the time, but painful. Later on, however,
it produces a harvest of righteousness and peace for those
who have been trained by it. Therefore, strengthen your
feeble arms and weak knees. "Make level paths for your
feet," so that the lame may not be disabled, but rather
healed.* [Hebrews 12:1-13, NIV]

Also, try working with some of the following verses with
your disciple:*Seek the LORD and his strength, seek his face
continually.* [I Chronicles 16:11, KJV]

*Though he fall, he shall not be utterly cast down: for the
LORD upholdeth him with his hand.* [Psalms 37:24, KJV]
*And I will make an everlasting covenant with them, that I will
not turn away from them, to do them good; but I will put my fear
in their hearts, that they shall not depart from me.* [Jeremiah 32:40,
KJV]

*But he that shall endure unto the end, the same shall be saved.* [Matthew 24:13, KJV]

*And this is the will of him who sent me, that I shall lose none of all that he has given me, but raise them up at the last day. For my Father's will is that everyone who looks to the Son and believes in him shall have eternal life, and I will raise him up at the last day."* [John 6:39-40, NIV]

*Abide in me, and I in you. As the branch cannot bear fruit of itself, except it abide in the vine; no more can ye, except ye abide in me. I am the vine, ye are the branches: He that abideth in me, and I in him, the same bringeth forth much fruit: for without me ye can do nothing. If ye abide in me, and my words abide in you, ye shall ask what ye will, and it shall be done unto you.* [John 15:4-5 & 7, KJV]

*"As the Father has loved me, so have I loved you. Now remain in my love."* [John 15:9, NIV]

*And when they had preached the gospel to that city, and had taught many, they returned again to Lystra, and to Iconium, and Antioch, confirming the souls of the disciples, and exhorting them to continue in the faith, and that we must through much tribulation enter into the kingdom of God.* [Acts 14:21-22, KJV]

*God "will give to each person according to what he has done." To those who by persistence in doing good seek glory, honor and immortality, he will give eternal life.*
[Romans 2:6-7, NIV]

*No, in all these things we are more than conquerors through him who loved us.*
[Romans 8:37, NIV]

*Moreover, brethren, I declare unto you the gospel which I preached unto you, which also ye have received, and wherein ye stand; By which also ye are saved, if ye keep in memory what I preached unto you, unless ye have believed in vain.* [I Corinthians 15:1-2, KJV]

*Therefore, my dear brothers, stand firm. Let nothing move you. Always give yourselves fully to the work of the Lord, because you know that your labor in the Lord is not in vain.* [I Corinthians 15:58, NIV]

*Be on the alert, stand firm in the faith, act like men, be strong.* [I Corinthians 16:13, NASB]

*And he died for all, that those who live should no longer live for themselves but for him who died for them and was raised again.* [II Corinthians 5:15, NIV]

*It is for freedom that Christ has set us free. Stand firm, then, and do not let yourselves be burdened again by a yoke of slavery.* [Galatians 5:1, NIV]

*Then we will no longer be infants, tossed back and forth by the waves, and blown here and there by every wind of teaching and by the cunning and craftiness of men in their deceitful scheming. Instead, speaking the truth in love, we will in all things grow up into him who is the Head, that is, Christ.* [Ephesians 4:14-15, NIV]

*Therefore, my brethren dearly beloved and longed for, my joy and crown, so stand fast in the Lord, my dearly beloved.* [Philippians 4:1, KJV]

*And although you were formerly alienated and hostile in mind, engaged in evil deeds, yet He has now reconciled you in His fleshly body through death, in order to present you before Him holy and blameless and beyond reproach—if indeed you continue in the faith firmly established and steadfast, and not moved away from the hope of the gospel that you have heard, which was proclaimed in all creation under heaven, and of which I, Paul, was made a minister.* [Colossians 1:21-23, NASB]

*Rooted and built up in him, and established in the faith, as ye have been taught, abounding therein with thanksgiving.* [Colossians 2:7, KJV]

*For now we live, if ye stand fast in the Lord.* [II Thessalonians 3:8, KJV]

*Test everything. Hold on to the good. Avoid every kind of evil. May God himself, the God of peace, sanctify you through and through. May your whole spirit, soul and body be kept blameless at the coming of our Lord Jesus Christ. The one who calls you is faithful and he will do it.* [I Thessalonians 5:21, NIV]

*Therefore, brethren, stand fast, and hold the traditions which ye have been taught, whether by word, or our epistle. Now our Lord Jesus Christ himself, and God, even our Father, which hath loved us, and hath given us everlasting consolation and good hope through grace, Comfort your hearts, and establish you in every good word and work.* [II Thessalonians 2:15-17, KJV]

*For the which cause I also suffer these things: nevertheless I am not ashamed: for I know whom I have believed, and am persuaded that he is able to keep that which I have committed unto him against that day. Hold fast the form of sound words, which thou hast heard of me, in faith and love which is in Christ Jesus.* [II Timothy 1:12-13, KJV]

*Endure hardship with us like a good soldier of Christ Jesus. No one serving as a soldier gets involved in civilian affairs—he wants to please his commanding officer.* [II Timothy 2:3-4, NIV]

*If we suffer, we shall also reign with him: if we deny him, he also will deny us.* [II Timothy 2:12, KJV]

*But continue thou in the things which thou hast learned and hast been assured of, knowing of whom thou hast learned them.* [II Timothy 3:14, KJV]

*And the Lord shall deliver me from every evil work, and will preserve me unto his heavenly kingdom: to whom be glory for ever and ever. Amen.* [II Timothy 4:18, KJV]

*Moses was faithful as a servant in all God's house, testifying to what would be said in the future. But Christ is faithful as a son over God's house. And we are his house, if we hold on to our courage and the hope of which we boast.* [Hebrews 3:5-6, NIV]

*For we are made partakers of Christ, if we hold the beginning of our confidence steadfast unto the end;* [Hebrews 3:14, KJV]

*Seeing then that we have a great high priest, that is passed into the heavens, Jesus the Son of God, let us hold fast our profession.* [Hebrews 4:14, KJV]

*And so, after he had patiently endured, he obtained the promise.* [Hebrews 6:15, KJV]

*Let us hold fast the confession of our hope without wavering, for He who promised is faithful; and let us consider how to stimulate one another to love and good deeds, not forsaking our own assembling together, as is the habit of some, but encouraging one another; and all the more as you see the day drawing near.* [Hebrews 10:23-25, NASB]

*Therefore, do not throw away your confidence, which has a great reward. For you have need of endurance, so that when you have done the will of God, you may receive what was promised.* [Hebrews 10:35-36, NASB]

*Keep your lives free from the love of money and be content with what you have, because God has said, "Never will I leave you; never will I forsake you. So we say with confidence, "The Lord is my helper; I will not be afraid. What can man do to me?" Remember your leaders, who spoke the word of God to you. Consider the outcome of their way of life and imitate their faith. Jesus Christ is the same yesterday and today and forever. Do not be carried away by all kinds of strange teachings. It is good for our hearts to be strengthened by grace, not by ceremonial foods, which are of no value to those who eat them.* [Hebrews 13:5-10, NIV]

*But let patience have her perfect work, that ye may be perfect and entire, wanting nothing.* [James 1:4, KJV]

*Blessed is a man who perseveres under trial; for once he has been approved, he will receive the crown of life which the Lord has promised to those who love Him* [James 1:12, KJV]

*But one who looks intently at the perfect law, the law of liberty, and abides by it, not having become a forgetful hearer but an effectual doer, this man will be blessed in what he does.* [James 1:25, NASB]

*Take, my brethren, the prophets, who have spoken in the name of the Lord, for an example of suffering affliction, and of patience. Behold, we count them happy which endure. Ye have heard of the patience of Job, and have seen the end of the Lord; that the Lord is very pitiful, and of tender mercy.* [James 5:10-11, KJV]

*Blessed be the God and Father of our Lord Jesus Christ, who according to His great mercy has caused us to be born again to a living hope through the resurrection of Jesus Christ from the dead, to obtain an inheritance which is imperishable and undefiled and will not fade away, reserved in heaven for you, who are protected by the power of God through faith for a salvation ready to be revealed in the last time. In this you greatly rejoice, even though now for a little while, if necessary, you have been distressed by various trials, so that the proof of your faith, being more precious than gold which is perishable, even though tested by fire, may be found to result in praise and glory and honor at the revelation of Jesus Christ; and though you have not seen Him, you love Him, and though you do not see Him now, but believe in Him, you greatly rejoice with joy inexpressible and full of glory, obtaining as the outcome of your faith the salvation of your souls.* [II Peter 1:4-9, NASB]

*Be sober, be vigilant; because your adversary the devil, as a roaring lion, walketh about, seeking whom he may devour:* [II Peter 5:8, KJV]

*Therefore, brethren, be all the more diligent to make certain about His calling and choosing you; for as long as you practice these things, you will never stumble; for in this way the entrance into the eternal kingdom of our Lord and Savior Jesus Christ will be abundantly supplied to you.* [II Peter 1:10-11, NASB]

*Therefore, dear friends, since you already know this, be on your guard so that you may not be carried away by the error of lawless men and fall from your secure position. But grow in the grace and knowledge of our Lord and Savior Jesus Christ. To him be glory both now and forever! Amen.* [II Peter 3:17-18, NIV]

*He that hath an ear, let him hear what the Spirit saith unto the churches; To him that overcometh will I give to eat of the tree of life, which is in the midst of the paradise of God.* [Revelation 2:7, KJV]

*He that hath an ear, let him hear what the Spirit saith unto the churches; To him that overcometh will I give to eat of the hidden manna, and will give him a white stone, and in the stone a new name written, which no man knoweth saving he that receiveth it.* [Revelation 2:17, KJV]

*To him who overcomes and does my will to the end, I will give authority over the nations— He will rule them with an iron scepter; he will dash them to pieces like pottery just as I have received authority from my Father. I will also give him the morning star.* [Revelation 2:25-28, KJV]

*He who overcomes will, like them, be dressed in white. I will never blot out his name from the book of life, but will acknowledge his name before my Father and his angels.* [Revelation 3:5, NIV]

*I am coming soon. Hold on to what you have, so that no one will take your crown. Him who overcomes I will make a pillar in the temple of my God. Never again will he leave it. I will write on him the name of my God and the name of the city of my God, the new Jerusalem, which is coming down out of heaven from my God; and I will also write on him my new name.* [Revelation 3:11-12, NIV]

*To him that overcometh will I grant to sit with me in my throne, even as I also overcame, and am set down with my Father in his throne.* [Revelation 3:21, KJV]

*Here is the patience of the saints: here are they that keep the commandments of God, and the faith of Jesus.* [Revelation 14:12, KJV]

My personal favorite verse for any Soil Type Three person I meet is also my favorite verse for me:

*No, in all these things we are more than conquerors through him who loved us. For I am convinced that neither death nor life, neither angels nor demons, neither the present nor the future, nor any powers, neither height nor depth, nor anything else in all creation, will be able to separate us from the love of God that is in Christ Jesus our Lord.* [Romans 8:37-39, KJV]

Now go read the essay in Addendum C.

## Chapter Nine

# SOIL TYPE FOUR

*"Others, like seed sown on good soil, hear the word, accept it, and produce a crop—thirty, sixty or even a hundred times what was sown."*

And the fourth soil type is really exciting. As a discipler, you can't say or do anything without that person just looking for an opportunity to apply it. There is an excitement and zeal to that person which seems to infect everything around them, including the discipler. The Samaritan "Woman at the Well" is an excellent example of this Soil Type Four.

Let's take a moment and look more closely at that heavenly appointment. You have probably heard many sermons and teachings about this particular meeting, but allow me to share my own perspective for a moment.

I mentioned this earlier, but I think it needs to be examined again. So here is what happened, sort of... from John 4:6-39, sort of...

Jesus had a very busy time ministering all over Judea. Then he headed north toward Galilee, passing through what was known as Samaria. He found himself at Jacob's Well, a large and very important well where many people came from miles around to get water. Normally, the water was obtained by women very early in the morning, when it was cool and before all the meals and chores of the day. They drew water, poured it into large pots, and then carried the pots back home every morning. But Jesus showed up about noon, knowing in advance there was a chance that no one would be at the well for possibly hours. He sent his disciples into town for Chinese take-out, and he sat down and rested. Or some would say he waited.

Finally, a Samaritan woman showed up at the well. As you probably know, Samaritans were considered half-breed Jews and traitors to the Jewish people, and even the Jewish God. Samaritans were descendants of Jews who were captured and taken to Babylon hundreds of years earlier, along with Daniel, Shadrach, Meshach, and Abednego. (You can read their stories in the Book of Daniel.) The Babylonians, when they conquered a city or a civilization, would take young leadership-oriented men and women back to Babylon and feed them into the culture there. Once these people were "trained" (an early application of brainwashing...) in new attitudes and perspectives, they were sent back to their homes as a way of spreading the Babylonian culture. Naturally, while in Babylon, many of the Jews would adopt the social and even the religious customs of the Babylonians, and many would marry Babylonian spouses. All this helped ensure that there would be no long-term military backlash to the Babylonian invasion efforts; with the young leadership of the conquered nation believing in and practicing Babylonian ways and culture, there was reduced chance of a revenge attack.

The problem was when those Jews came back home to Israel. They were considered traitors and half-breeds and were treated as ceremonially unclean by the "true" Jews. So these transplanted Jews were definitely not accepted back into Jewish culture and society. As a result, they settled in Samaria and pretty much kept to themselves.

And it was a Samaritan woman who showed up at the well with Jesus sitting there. She was at the well getting water around noon because she would have received all sorts of abuse from the Samaritan women had she arrived early in the morning hours with most of the women. Jesus was there after a hard morning's work, so he asked for a drink of water. We all know what happened next.

When the Samaritan woman rushed home to talk to her family and friends about Jesus, a common reaction when people meet Jesus for the first time, the disciples came back to Jacob's Well with lunch. Jesus told them, *"I have meat to eat that you know not of."* [John 4:32, KJV] The disciples were confused, asking each other if Domino's delivered pizza way out at the well, or something like that. *"Hath any man brought him ought to eat?"* [John 4:33, KJV] And Jesus explained to them that when we minister to others, we are spiritually fed and we spiritually grow.

This is a principle that the discipler will experience over and over again. When we reach out and minister the Word of God to others, teaching them and discipling them, we will experience an infusion of spiritual food and spiritual growth ourselves. One simply cannot touch others in the name of Jesus without personal spiritual benefit.

And this is especially obvious when we are dealing with Soil Type Four people.

There is a zeal and excitement to the Type Four Soil that is tangible and contagious. The discipler often finds he or she experiences periods of personal spiritual growth when working with a Soil Type Four person unlike anything the discipler experiences elsewhere. This is how God has designed things. Taking on the responsibility of discipling another Believer is often difficult and always taxing. And to make up for the emotional (and sometimes physical) drain on the discipler, God has planned a sort of compensation for the discipler - personal spiritual food and growth.

## *Your Strategy:*

With Soil Type Four people, you need to feed their zeal. There is little more to do. Just make sure you continue to feed their thirst for knowledge. These people already want to know God, so you just help them to know God better. Take them through a series of Scripture verses that challenge them to grow. These people already have a natural desire to UNDERSTAND, so give them things to understand. It would not hurt to take a Bible Dictionary or a Bible Handbook and look up topics to teach on and challenge them with. You provide a topic or an issue and offer them a few Bible verses. Then ask a few questions, especially using the word WHY, and watch them dig.

## *Their Weaknesses:*

If they have any weaknesses, it is to go off "half-cocked" or jump to conclusions without enough study. Their excitement will be contagious, but also a problem. They will often sound as if they know more than they actually do, so be careful to take the time to discern if they really do understand what they seem to understand.

## *Assignments for Soil Type Four:*

Background materials will always be in order so they can understand the _WHY_ of a particular passage or a particular response of those hearing Jesus teach. I have found that maps are always worth studying – it is good to see where things happened or how far Jesus had to walk to get someplace. The distance traveled often adds insight into events. For example, in Christ's early ministry, people followed Jesus all over town. In his later years, people often walked for hours just to see him and hear him teach. Facts like how far it was from Capernaum to the north shore of the Sea of Galilee or how far it was from

Jerusalem to Samaria can often add additional meaning to events. A question that I have often discovered that is not understood by many people is why Scripture always refers to "going down" to Jerusalem. People usually say because Jerusalem is south of Galilee. But why does Scripture refer to going down to Jerusalem even when the person was heading north? Another point to consider is who lived in the area Jesus was teaching or performing miracles. When Jesus cast the demons out of the herd of pigs (the first case of deviled ham in history), you see that Jesus was not in an area inhabited by Jews, but by a mix of races and political perspectives. This had to be true because Jews would never raise pigs! This is not clear from just Scripture - you have to take the time to read in a Bible Dictionary who lived in the area that Scripture called the Decapolis.

If they are new enough to Scripture that they do not understand much about the time of Christ, the use of Bible Dictionaries and Bible Encyclopedias is worth the time and expense. Controversial doctrines can be used effectively to challenge these people to dig deeper into the things of God, adding to their understanding. Superficial treatment of issues like Eternal Security and the Baptism of the Holy Spirit can demotivate these people from growing in their understanding of theological issues. Take them deeper!

Make extensive use of "homework" to challenge these people. And don't be afraid to give them time to effectively study the issues. A week or two is not a long time to study some of the issues with which God will lead you to challenge them. And the more time you can spend with them, the better they will learn to apply what they are studying.

Consider picking a Gospel and studying it with them. Developing a good handle on the chronology of Christ's ministry is beneficial for every Christian to learn. If you are not sure which Gospel to select, I recommend the Gospel According to Mark. Further, try comparing and contrasting how the different Gospel writers reported events - this will lead to a deeper understanding of the personalities of the men Jesus gathered around him. Each of the Gospel writers was different – feel free to explore *why* they were different.

This is true of all the people in the Bible. Pick some prominent people and spend some time searching through all the references to them. And pick some people from both the *Old* and *New Testament*. Don't be afraid to spend a lot of time in the *Old Testament*. Most Christians tend to spend very little time in the *Old Testament*, giving them a very shallow and incomplete knowledge of the Jews and the customs of the people Jesus grew up around. It is always a good thing to understand the heritage and society that gave Jesus his roots.

With Soil Type Four people, specific Scripture verses become less important than the issues and concepts that form the basis for our life in Christ. So be prepared to spend quite a bit of time discussing what many Christians describe with disdain as "theology." Just remember that commentaries are merely someone's opinion about Scripture. They may be knowledgeable, but they are still human.

Voltaire, a French philosopher and atheist who became a Christian convert, once said, *"Judge a man not by his answers but by his questions."* Soil Type Four people ask a lot of questions. Don't be afraid of questions to which you may not know the answers. Use them to stretch your own knowledge and the knowledge of your disciples. If you don't know the answer to a particular question, respond with something like, "I don't know the answer. Why don't we research it together?" You will find that Soil Type Four people are more impressed with your willingness to learn *WITH* them than your ability to *TEACH* them.

These people usually want to learn. All you have to do is provide some questions and turn them loose. Just be prepared with some sort of agenda. And then be prepared for the ride of your life!

If you doubt your expertise in studying the Bible, I have written a book about a particular Bible study method called Inductive Bible Study. It is available on Amazon.com.

In _Addendum D_, you will find an essay written for some Soil Type Four people I knew. It provides a simple tactic for keeping your eyes on Christ as you strive to be more like him in your daily life.

## Chapter Ten

# CONCLUSION

I believe that discipling other Believers is the most exciting and fulfilling activity that any Believer can enjoy. This is especially true when the discipler is working with a Believer who is spiritually prepared and ready to grow and bear fruit. There is nothing like the joy of sowing God's Living Word into the lives of others, especially if those others are Soil Type Four people.

Yes, there is spiritual reward in sowing to Soil Type One; not so much because of a Soil Type One individual, but because there is always spiritual reward for doing the work of Jesus. And yes, there is even more spiritual reward and spiritual food and spiritual joy in sowing the Living Word of God into Soil Types Two and Three. But there is *nothing* like the experience of sowing the Living Word of God into Soil Type Four.

When a discipler is working with Soil Types Two and Three, the effort should be in soil preparation more than anything else. For once the discipler gets a disciple into the proper soil condition, then the energy that comes out of the experience becomes self-sustaining. The discipler finds no higher joy than ministering to Soil Type Four person.

Again, we have to ask how does a discipler discern which soil type is before him or her? The discipler must become a fruit inspector.

Soil Type Two received the Living Word of God with joy and eagerness, but there is no real root system. Without a root system developed deep into the Word, these people are especially susceptible to spiritual persecution. Even simple questions like, "*Do you really believe that?*" produce doubts and concerns. Without any real root system, that soil type can *FEEL* no real answers, and the doubts and concerns and fears soon overwhelm them. The Believer then often chokes and withers.

Soil Type Three people experience some degree of growth. But those people do not understand the things of God well enough to balance the new life with the old life, new responsibilities with old responsibilities, new interests with old interests. The result is again predictable: confusion, floundering, little or no growth, and no fruit.

How does the discipler discern the stumbling blocks to spiritual growth in a disciple? It is simple: look at what is getting in the way. The Soil Types Two and Three disciples will almost always manifest the stumbling blocks as clearly as Soil Type Four people manifest the fruit. As a discipler, ask questions about the basics of the Christian life; questions about time spent in prayer, in the Word, in church; questions about how they applied the last lesson to their life. The new Believer will give answers that show their stumbling blocks quite clearly.

But you need to ask questions relative to the root system.

Notice again the issue in the parable. The real issue is the root system; the basics. The Soil Type allows for a specific root system with specific weaknesses which result in specific problems. Soil Type One has no sprouts and no roots. Soil Type Two has sprouts but no roots. Soil Type Three has poor plants because of poor roots. Soil Type Four has great roots resulting in great plants and awesome fruit.

Asking questions that require any real understanding of the Bible will often give false or misleading indicators. Even Soil Type One can give accurate answers if he or she grew up in a conservative church with good teaching.

And as you evaluate the answers you are getting from the questions you are asking, you will often be able to discern quite easily the impediments, and therefore the Soil Type. And then you can design a discipleship strategy best suited to the soil type and the individual.

Soil Type Two is filled with doubts and concerns, even fears. The solution is not to teach spiritual facts and truths as much as it is to LOVE THEM.

*"There is no fear in love. But perfect love drives out fear, because fear has to do with punishment."* [I John 4:18, NIV]

This person really needs to put to rest the concept of the love and forgiveness of our Heavenly Father. Help them experience the security of his love and acceptance as they never experienced it before. Once they have experienced the love and acceptance by you and by God, you can teach them all about God's forgiveness, and the changed life they can expect as a result of that forgiveness. It is easy to go from milk to meat, but only after their fears are laid to rest.

Soil Type Two needs to be able to rest in the love and forgiveness of God.

Soil Type Three is not so much a result of fear as it is a failure to balance. This is a function primarily of experience, or lack thereof. After living their entire lives under an ungodly system of values and morals, now they are faced with living in that same world but with godly values and morals. For most of us, we need to see someone do it before we can even understand the problem, much less beat the problem. Soil Type Three usually needs a role model more than Biblical teaching. A discipler who knows how to balance a godly lifestyle within an ungodly world philosophy will be an immeasurable help to a Soil Type Three disciple. If a discipler can successfully walk with God and still be a success in this worldly system, that discipler can turn a Soil Type Three disciple into a Soil Type Four disciple more quickly than one might expect.

Mortgages, day care, budgets, entertainment, family time and personal time are only a few of the many major issues demanding time and attention from a Soil Type Three disciple. All Believers face these same pressures, but Soil Type Three people seem to have a particular inability to balance everything. And most likely that disciple has never seen any other Believer effectively balance these and other demands with any type of spiritual life.

Give the disciple a success story -- _BE A SUCCESS STORY_ -- and you will change your disciple's life for an eternity. Chances are that is all the disciple needs.

So let's make this simple.

Build yourself a chart. Make three vertical columns, and as many horizontal rows as you have disciples. At the top of the left-hand column, put the heading of NAME. At the top of the middle column, put the heading of FRUIT. At the top of the right-hand column put the heading of FARMING.

The left-hand column is a list of your disciples. You might list only one disciple at a time, and complete the next two columns on that disciple before going on the next one. The middle column is for you to list the fruit that you see in the disciple's life - fruit of the Spirit and fruit of ministry. The right-hand column is for you to list all the reasons why other fruit, or more fruit, are not obvious from this disciple.

The middle column requires that you judge your disciple, that you assess spiritual strengths and weaknesses, that you become an effective fruit inspector. The middle column requires that you _KNOW_ your disciple.

And the right-hand column is where you BEGIN writing down what you believe God wants you to build into the life of the disciple. Notice I said "build into" rather than teach. You do not need to know a lot of Scripture or a lot of theology in order to build great disciples; you only need to walk with God and want to share that with others.

As you can see, being a discipler of your Soil Type Two and Soil Type Three disciples is quite simple, but not at all easy. The basic function of the discipler with either Soil Type is to spend time with the disciple, transferring certain aspects of your life into the life of the disciple. Soil Type Two disciples need certain things from the discipler, and Soil Type Three disciples need different things from the discipler.  But both soil types need to _see_ it in order to _do_ it.

Being an effective discipler is not a function of picking the absolute best set of printed teaching materials available on the Internet or at the local Christian Bookstore.  Being an effective discipler has nothing to do with choosing the proper Bible translation or singing the right Christian music.  Being an effective discipler is a function of building the Living Word of God from your life into the lives of disciples.

The important part of being a great discipler is not what you know - _it is what you are!_  You impart the life of God, YOUR LIFE with God, into the life of a new disciple.  Use books, use teaching materials, use Bible verse memorization, use anything that helps the disciple see and know Jesus better.  But most importantly, use your own life.  As you walk with God, you will find your disciple walks with God alongside you.

And knowing the Soil Types helps you fine tune both your discipling and your disciple.

For the last few pages we have been looking at discipleship and what is involved, even required, of a Believer involved in a discipleship relationship with another Believer.  While we have considered the process of discipleship, and the results of discipleship, we have not proposed any definitions of the relevant issues.

As we have seen, Jesus commands all Believers to be involved in discipleship to some extent.

> _All authority in heaven and on earth has been given to me. Therefore go into all the world and make disciples of all nations, baptizing them in the name of the Father and of the Son and of the Holy Spirit, and teaching them to obey everything I have commanded you. "_  [Matthew 28:18-21, NIV]

Concerning Scripture, someone has said, "When you see the word _therefore_, you need to see what the word is there for."

So let's look more closely at something that might have escaped some of us.

Jesus here just proclaimed himself to be the owner and ruler and boss of the entire universe. He didn't just say that he had more POWER than anyone else. He wasn't making the childhood claim that *"My dad can beat up your dad."* Jesus was saying that he had more AUTHORITY than anyone else. To paraphrase that childhood claim, he said, *"My dad can have your dad arrested and executed."*

Jesus claimed all authority in the universe, and then he immediately said, *"Go."* We know that Jesus gave what we call the *Great Commission* to his eleven disciples. It appears that there may have been additional disciples or serious followers of his in the room also, but some learned men have disputed this. But it seems clear that ONLY serious followers of Christ were there, whatever the number. Jesus gave the command to committed Believers; not to the world, and not to casual Believers.

So we can conclude that all who are committed to following Jesus are subject to this command.

Jesus claimed to have the authority to command every living being in the universe, and then he gave a command to his committed followers.

What was the relationship between the authority of Jesus and the command of Jesus? Apart from the obvious, the question demands a long and detailed response that would involve more theology than this short book on discipleship would warrant. So we will leave this question for another essay.

Suffice it to say that Jesus just claimed the authority to command every human on the planet. And then he delivered a command to only those Believers who are serious about following him.

And what was that command which Jesus gave to his disciples?

*"Go and make disciples."* Not *"Go and share the Gospel,"* but *"Go and make disciples."*

So it is time for me offer some definitions.

**gnosis**: knowledge; an intellectual awareness of a certain set of facts

**epignosis**: experience; knowledge that has been learned and then proven through firsthand experience

**teaching**: imparting gnosis

**training**: leading someone from gnosis into epignosis

Let's see how these definitions apply to discipleship.

Discipleship is the process of one Believer imparting the gnosis of God on a continuing basis so as to assist the disciple in his or her efforts at turning gnosis into epignosis.

Or we can simplify it a little more.

**Discipleship is the process of one Believer teaching and then training other Believers to understand and then to apply Scripture so they can live more like Jesus over time.**

Discipleship includes:
TEACHING Scripture such that the disciple believes and understands that all thoughts and all actions serve either God or Satan; and
TRAINING the disciple in the effective application of Scriptural concepts and Biblical tools to the life of the disciple such that he or she becomes more like Christ over time

And we must remember what Paul claimed to one of his primary disciples:

*All Scripture is God-breathed and is useful for teaching, rebuking, correcting and training in righteousness, so that the man of God may be thoroughly equipped for every good work.* [II Timothy 3:16, NIV]

116

The Believer has two primary tools for use in discipling other Believers. First, he or she imparts biblical teaching as he or she gains spiritual insight into walking with God. Second, he or she imparts from personal experience to the disciple how to turn simple Scriptural principles into daily living.

In other words, as I study Scripture with an open heart, the Holy Spirit guides me into more and more truth concerning how Jesus lived and how he wants me to live. I can then share with my disciples what I am learning and how I am changing. This will build the life of Christ into them.

As Paul stated in his first letter to the Church at Thessalonica:

> *For we know, brothers loved by God, that he has chosen you, because our gospel came to you not simply with words, but also with power, with the Holy Spirit and with deep conviction. You know how we lived among you for your sake. You became imitators of us and of the Lord; in spite of severe suffering, you welcomed the message with joy given by the Holy Spirit. And you became a model to all the Believers in Macedonia and Achaia.* [I Thessalonians 1:4-7, NIV]

It is the heartfelt desire of all Christ-centered disciplers that we live in such a way that our lives affect and infect our disciples and that they become imitators of us and of the Lord we serve and so that they become a model of Jesus to others.

> *We have not stopped praying for you and asking God to fill you with the knowledge [Gr-epignosis, experiential knowledge] of his will through all spiritual wisdom and understanding. And we pray this in order that you may live a life worthy of the Lord and may please him in every way: bearing fruit in every good work, growing in the knowledge of God, being strengthened with all power according to his glorious might so that you may have great endurance and patience, and joyfully giving thanks to the Father, who has qualified you to share in the*

*inheritance of the saints in the kingdom of light.* [Colossians 1:9-12, NIV]

This, my brothers and sisters, is discipleship.

# ADDENDUM A

## *An Essay for Soil Type One*

Many Soil Type One people tend to see themselves as intellectuals, and as more intelligent and more open than most people. So they read everything and study much in order to pursue a greater knowledge [*Gr-gnosis, collection of facts*] of God. They honestly believe that the more they know *ABOUT* God, the greater their understanding *OF* God. And the more they read and study, the more views and opinions about God they gather. As a result, they are constrained by their regard for knowledge to accept more and more views of God than their initial understanding of God allows. Since knowledge is to be sought after, it is presumed that knowledge cannot be disregarded. But in their zeal to amass knowledge about God, they are confronted with the discrepancies between the differing views of God. Hence, they are forced to establish some ground rules in the pursuit of God. In other words, they tend to develop their own personal views of God, and see others, especially Christians, as limited in their understanding.

# *Religious Delusions*

One of the many possible examples of Soil Type One in the *Parable of the Sower* (or, as I believe it should be called, the *Parable of the Soils*) is the intellectual person who considers himself to be just too open-minded and inclusive to believe in the impossibly confining views and demands expressed in the Bible. And these so-called Intellectuals tend to look and sound the same. Please allow me to explain.

In psychological circles, one is often labeled as paranoid schizophrenic when one builds one or more delusions, or fictional worlds, within which one likes to dwell, or continually dwells, to the exclusion of what the rest of us call "reality." Some of these delusional worlds are intricately constructed, with unbelievably detailed parameters.

**In religious circles, we can see that exact same delusional world.**

Some of the symptoms, or traits, of a strong paranoid delusion include: 1) a clear "*we versus they*" duality with few, if any, on the "*we*" side and almost everyone else on the "*they*" side"; 2) an obvious but undefined set of rules for this delusional world; 3) others are expected to understand and follow these unwritten rules or the individual may become agitated or even upset; 4) those who do not know the rules without being told them, who do not spontaneously obey these rules without any explanation, are quickly judged as being deficient or inferior in some way; 5) a developing or evolving story line; 6) "facts" to support the delusion are taken from many sources, even diametrically opposed sources, but nearly always taken out of context so they can be misconstrued or misrepresented more easily; 7) and the underlying presumptions, sometimes even the primary beliefs, are seldom conscious beliefs, with the delusional individual often unaware of them.

Unfortunately, a strong religious delusion shares almost all the same symptoms.

Those holding religious delusions sound like they are open-minded, even claim to be open-minded. They tend to use the word inclusive, and gently, often with a smile of condescension, will suggest that those who are not inclusive have a ways to go in their emotional and mental and philosophical growth. Phrases like, "I used to believe that, too" sprinkle their discussions. And these people usually believe, and often suggest, that the more varied their sources, and the more inclusive their beliefs, the more virtue in their beliefs.

The purpose for this essay is not to outline a strategy to change or "convert" these people. The people who maintain these religious delusions are usually quite firm in their beliefs, and are seldom open to changing them. Any discussion or debate of the issues is fun for the intellectual exercise, but normally doomed to frustrating all the individuals involved. In other words, argument is probably a waste of time. Further, argument will almost always degrade to personal insults and subjective perspectives. If the delusional individual cannot clearly win the debate, then he or she will side-track the debate and move down personal paths. Beware – you may become the target of the debate.

Now let's look at the Parable again. And please note: One must keep in mind the description of Soil Type One given by Jesus:

> *Some people are like the seed along the path, where the word is sown. As soon as they hear it, Satan comes and takes away the word that was sown in them.* [Mark 4:15, NIV]

Jesus DID NOT say, "Don't waste your time with them." But Jesus DID tell us what will result from our discussions with this type of person.

Allow me to offer some definitions for the purpose of our discussion:

**Christian** - one who perceives himself or herself to be a follower of Jesus as the Christ, the Messiah, to the exclusion of all other religious leaders; one who perceives the Bible as the primary religious text concerning Jesus

**Evangelical Christian** - a Christian who perceives himself or herself to be on the conservative side of the collection of individuals claiming to be Christians; one who believes that the life, death, and resurrection of Jesus are firmly established historical and spiritual facts; one who believes that the Bible is inspired by God in the original texts and TRUTH for all Christians

*Bible* - a collection of writings involving dozens of writers over thousands of years, all collected into a document that was and is inspired by God and accurate in the original texts; a "book" that exists today only in translation, which is just that: the result of sincere people performing a careful process of translation using what they believed to be the best texts available to them; the major translations today being so similar in text that the differences are more in the depths and nuances of meaning than in real or practical meaning of the words; does not include some later attempts to "translate" based on a clear and usually stated attempt to change the meaning of older translations to conform more to the current social and religious beliefs of a minority of people who may not even call themselves Christians (e.g. a certain "modern translation" by a well-known science fiction author to render God either female or gender-neutral)

Over the years, I have found myself put in the position of dialoging, even debating, with quite a number of people who refer to themselves as Christians earlier in their lives but later in life tended to pull back from that statement. They have all been quite intelligent and well-read. And they have all tended to embrace the fairly common belief that all major religions teach the same core "truths" and worship the same God by one name or another. Whether or not they choose to admit it, they all consider themselves intellectual and believe themselves to be unique. But within their ranks, they are all quite similar.

I have always valued these people and these discussions, not so much because I saw any victory in pushing or pulling the other individual in any given spiritual direction, but because I valued the refreshing and stimulating thought processes involved in these often intense discussions. One must be an original thinker in order to swim upstream against the current, and I will always appreciate an original thinker. But from these discussions, I have observed some similarities in those thought processes that I thought I might put forth, evidence that not ALL their thinking is original. And I have decided to write about why I believe at least *some* of those thought processes are inherently wrong, internally inconsistent, and even intellectually dishonest.

You see, these thought processes, these religious delusions, are all a closed world, self-reinforcing, and accountable to ONLY the subjective realities of those who live in them.

Please understand that I am not saying that any of the individuals were dishonest, but that certain similarities in the thought processes and logic of these people tend toward internal inconsistency and even intellectual dishonesty. In truth, I believe that each of these people were engaged in a spiritual delusion of monumental importance, and most were not aware of this fact. In fact, few of these people would believe such a claim.

As an example, one man I knew and who suffered from this religious delusion syndrome believed that Jesus was a good man who came to earth as a servant to mankind. Theologians refer to this belief as the "Suffering Servant" role of Jesus. And this man was quick to offer a Scripture verse to anyone who would listen to him describing his belief that Jesus came as a "suffering servant" with the purpose of helping, even improving, all humanity. Of course, there was no need to repent of any sins in this man's world, because Jesus loved everyone too much to demand anything from them. Instead, Jesus himself would be a servant to everyone and slowly but surely improve all mankind that was open to this improvement. All who were not open to this improvement were either narrow-minded or too selfish to improve and serve others. The goal of Jesus, the goal of all of life, and especially the goal of all religions, was to love and serve others.

And to support this view of Jesus and his purpose, he often made reference to one particular passage in Scripture:

*Jesus himself did not come to be served, but to serve others.*

This was the man's most frequently quoted verse from the Bible, and it was always offered as an explanation of his view of the life and purpose of Jesus. Of course, he always offered it without any reference to the chapter and verse from which he took the passage.

I confronted him one day when he was having a conversation with others where he again made that reference. I said, "Why don't you quote the entire verse instead of taking out of the verse only the few words you want others to believe?" And I quoted the entire verse for him and those listening.

*Just as the Son of Man did not come to be served, but to serve, and to give his life a ransom for many.* [Matthew 20:28, NIV]

I went on to say, "Jesus didn't come to do nice things for others. He came to DIE so your sins and mine can be forgiven. THAT was how Jesus served mankind. You aren't being honest about what Scripture says was the reason Jesus came to earth."

He looked surprised, almost shocked, at my words. I never knew if he was surprised at what the entire verse stated, or if he was surprised that I would suggest he wasn't being honest, or if he was surprised that I could quote the entire verse from memory. Either way, I never heard him reference that passage again in my presence.

Allow me to describe, to build, a delusion of my own for you to better understand this type of person and this type of religious delusion.

But first there are some ground rules that we must accept for our discussions, or we can go no further. This condition of mandated ground rules is the norm for all spiritual delusions I have encountered, although they are normally left unspoken until they were needed to defend the delusion.

First, there is a God, and there is only one God, but this God is NOT like any God or god worshiped in any of the well-known religious traditions; similar to all of them, but different from any of them. Instead, my God is more an amalgam of a number of these traditions. God is, after all, a representation of a particular religious perspective, but in reality the same God is worshiped by all. What you call _your_ God is merely your view of God from the position where you stand. Others are standing in different positions and see a slightly different view. It is pompous and prideful for you to claim that your view from your perspective is correct to the exclusion of all other views and perspectives. God is too great to be limited by any man's vision and understanding. I, of course, am NOT being pompous or prideful in claiming that my view of God is right, or at least is more accurate, than your view.

Second, God has chosen to reveal himself in many ways and to many groups of people. I accept the Bible and the words of Jesus as authoritative. I also accept other religious writings and other religious figures as authoritative. But we must acknowledge the proviso that the Bible we have today was written by many authors over thousands of years. We must understand that no effort of man is without flaws. We must allow that almost all biblical authors had little or no knowledge of the other authors, or of the other texts, and so had no opportunity to coordinate and cooperate with the messages of the other writers. As a result, the collection of stories and letters that is today accepted as the Bible must also be understood to be both incomplete and embellished. Incomplete because there is no reason to believe that God is finished inspiring authors to write more Scripture; embellished because scribes and translators over time have added snippets, and perhaps entire sections, in order to clarify what they believed was the intent and meaning of the original authors.

Third, I accept a long list of authors and teachers as authoritative about God – about who and what he is, what he is like, what he wants, and how to get to know him. I quote these authorities often in discussions of God and religious issues, and I expect you to have read these authorities and understand what they believe when we discuss these issues. If you cannot, then we both must accept that you can have very little of any importance to add to our discussion or to my beliefs. We both must accept that you are intellectually limited for purposes of our discussion. I will USUALLY listen to what you have to say, with some patience, but only with that proviso. I am, after all, a Christian, and Christians are if nothing else loving and open to others of a different belief.

Fourth, the only restriction to our discussion, and this is a major point that cannot be debated or negotiated, is the fact that no author or teacher viewed as a conservative Christian is accepted as authoritative unless only certain claims are allowed and other claims can be dismissed, at my sole discretion. Any author or teacher who once held a conservative Christian view of God and who has recently modified his views to be more open and inclusive is naturally considered to be more authoritative in his more recent views. All honest thinkers must be open to further enlightenment, and those who are not, those who have remained unchanging in their views over time, have limited content to add to our discussions and limited understanding of ultimate truth.

Fifth, the actual context of any biblical reference is insignificant. What Jesus said, or any biblical character has said, is the issue; who it was said to, what those listening actually believed the speaker meant, how they responded, what was going on before or during what was said - all are unimportant factors when it comes to interpreting the meaning of what was said and what we should "hear" from what was said. After all, if Hemingway's "*The Old Man and the Sea*" can have multiple meanings, something supposedly written by God can have unlimited meanings. Included in this ground rule is the fact that there is no TRUTH, no absolute, no "fact" that is true under any and all circumstances, or for all people. Everything in this life, especially everything in religious life, is subject to individual interpretation and to personal application in ways that might greatly vary from individual to individual, or from society to society.

And last, it is stipulated by all parties in any discussion that sources and claims which are contrary to those offered by Evangelical Christians are to be accepted as equally authoritative, and are acceptable as a complete and effective rebuttal to any claim or quote made by an Evangelical Christian, regardless of the source or of the beliefs of the source. A garbage collector has more authority in a discussion of these issues than Billy Graham as long as the garbage collector does not believe Jesus is God.

So what will our discussion sound like?

Just like every conversation I have had with a knowledgeable cynic who had the above perspectives on these issues.

No matter what is stated, one or more of the ground rules allows for a counter that can pretty much stop the conversation.

And what is really the purpose of those ground rules? It allows me to pick and choose what I believe and who I believe, and does not allow you to offer any argument that I cannot easily dismiss.

In fact, my favorite tactic is to counter a conservative argument with a quote from some famous person, usually someone with strongly stated spiritual views. He or she doesn't have to have any particular educational qualifications, just strongly stated views that are contrary to some conservative view stated by you. For example, you can make some claim about God and I could rebut your claim by quoting some politician or some actor, ANY politician or actor, who disagrees with your claim. And since any claim by anyone that is counter to any conservative claim is considered a credible claim, then my claim trumps your claim, and you cannot win.

My delusion is self-validating and self-reinforcing. No one can win any argument against me because I am in control of what is and what is not authoritative.

And the real issue is that I am in control. I decide what is right and wrong, who is right and wrong, what is acceptable and not acceptable. And often I do so by claiming that there IS no right and wrong. I get to control the argument. *And because I control the argument, I cannot lose the argument. **Ever.***

## **I have become the most powerful person in history -- I GET TO DEFINE TRUTH!**

While I will NEVER admit it, I have become my own idol. I have taken the position of God. I have defined TRUTH. My intellect has become the most important and most powerful force in the universe. NOTHING can be accepted as true unless I say it is true. In defense of this, I can quote more authorities than you. I can reference more books and authors and theologians than you. I can assume without proof that I MUST be right because I CAN reference more books and authors and theologians than you.

He who knows, wins.

And since I control who and what God is, I don't have to FEAR taking authority away from him. I don't have to FEAR making God a creation of mine.

I don't have to FEAR God!

The ONLY thing I have to fear is for you to understand the presuppositions and the stipulations of our discussion. I cannot admit to them, and you cannot delineate them. If at all possible, the presuppositions and stipulations MUST remain unspoken. And if anyone points them out, I will deny them. No matter how much I might have used any particular item above, I will deny believing that item or using that item.

I KNOW that the presuppositions and stipulations are totally unreasonable, totally illogical, and totally unfair. But my entire peace and confidence, *my entire life*, depends on those views. And it depends on those views remaining unspoken.

As long as you and I remain within the confines of all those unspoken presuppositions and stipulations, we can have a profitable and fruitful conversation.

After all, I am open-minded, right?

# ADDENDUM B

# *An Essay for Soil Type Two*

One characteristic of a Soil Type Two person is the need for spiritual pep rallies and other mountaintop or emotional experiences. The Soil Type Two person is initially excited about the Gospel and often manifests that excitement with the desire to see and participate in every gathering and concert and service possible. On the surface, that motivation seems quite spiritual. But if the Discipler looks deeper, he or she will see that the real motivation is spiritual excitement and spiritual affirmation. The Soil Type Two person doesn't pursue Jesus for the sake of knowing him better. He or she pursues Jesus because of the spiritual high he or she receives. But God doesn't want spiritual junkies, he wants disciples. The pursuit of Jesus for some reason other than to know him better often results in spiritual setbacks and even spiritual defeat.

# *Mountaintop Experiences*

I am tired of them. I don't want to go to them anymore. I won't participate in them again. I don't even want to hear from anyone else about them.

What am I talking about? Some people enjoy them as worship experiences. Others value them as mountaintop experiences. I call them Christian pep rallies. The pep rallies that so many churches and Christian groups hold in the name of God.

You know what I am talking about.

These pep rallies often center around top name Christian singing groups, all of which have a strong high tenor or a strong high soprano, or both, whose voices are quite powerful. A song starts out in a normal key so most of the audience can sing along. But each verse transitions into a higher key so that, after four or five verses, only a handful of tenors and sopranos in the country can sing that high and that strong. And then the final chord of the final verse is held so high and so strong and so long that it raises the hair on your arms and gives you goose bumps. When the song breaks, it leaves you so excited that you absolutely MUST shout something. So you shout something spiritual like everyone else around you. And just then the group starts another verse, often in an even higher key.

After a few of these songs, everyone is so emotionally jacked up that shouting spiritual words and phrases is almost impossible to resist.

And then the worship leader starts a slow, soft song, accompanied by some sort of announcement that *"the Holy Spirit is in this place."* The leader often says something like, *"Raise your hands if you can feel the presence of God."* Of course, nearly everyone can feel SOMETHING, so nearly everyone raises their hands. And the worship leader leads the audience through several verses of that slow song so that everyone gets the chance to *feel* God.

And often this whole process is repeated two or three times more, so everyone can go home claiming to have participated in such an awesome worship experience.

But was this truly a worship experience?

And if this was a worship experience, was it a good thing?

And if it was a good thing, was it a biblical experience?

Before I get burned at the stake for asking such questions and raising such doubts, let me make this clear: I LOVE THESE WORSHIP EXPERIENCES!!

131

I have attended them; I have sought them out on the radio; I own them on CDs and DVDs; I have even led these experiences myself.

But I have come to realize that they are often nothing more than an old-fashioned high school football pep rally, but with a spiritual emphasis. Pep rallies have a purpose; they aren't bad in and of themselves. *But they are pep rallies.* And their purpose, be it at a football game or at a Christian concert, is to get people excited.

I can, and HAVE, reproduced the same sort of feelings in myself and in others by using the same psychological gimmicks, but without any mention of Jesus.

During the fall of each year, the same level of emotional euphoria and near-hysteria is accomplished hundreds of times each week on high school and college campuses all over America.

Okay, I admit, I probably just made it impossible to avoid being burned at that stake by a mob of angry but sincere Christians.

But before I meet that stake, before you strike that match, I really need to ask the question few people ever want to answer: *WHY?*

Why do we need these emotionally manipulative Christian pep rallies?

Does God need them in order for the Holy Spirit to visit our worship experiences?

Or do these pep rallies primarily benefit the spiritual junkies who need still another "mountain-top experience?"

And is a *"mountain-top experience"* good for our spiritual lives?

As I said before, I LOVE these mountain-top experiences. I am, to some extent, a spiritual junkie myself. But I have to ask of myself and of others, *"Exactly what benefit do we receive from being emotionally jacked-up, even when it is done in a spiritual environment?"*

Maybe we should have started this article with a look at the mountain top experience that Jesus shared with some of his disciples. Perhaps we can get some clues as to the value of that type of high by looking at and listening to Jesus.

We can find the account of this mountaintop experience in Matthew 17:1-13, Mark 9:1-13, and Luke 9:27-36. All three accounts are virtually identical and all three accounts tell us of the same events preceding this experience: Jesus taught of his coming death; Jesus taught about us taking up our crosses and following him; and Jesus and his disciples took a week off. Then Jesus took Peter, James, and John up a mountain.

*There he was transfigured before them.* [Matthew 17:2, NIV]

While transfigured, Jesus walked around with Moses and Elijah for a while. And God put his seal of approval on this particular mountaintop experience by doing his Exodus cloud thing and saying,

*"This is my beloved Son, whom I love; with him I am well pleased. Listen to him!"* [Matthew 17:5, NIV]

Can you imagine anything more exciting than this? Think about it! You have witnessed Jesus healing people and casting out demons more times than you can remember. You were hand-picked by Jesus to be in his core group of disciples. And over the past few weeks and months, your role has developed into the primary disciple, Christ's main man! Then you get to see Jesus transfigured. You get to see Moses and Elijah alive and talking with Jesus. God shows up in a cloud like he did almost 2,000 years ago. AND GOD SPEAKS TO YOU!

And what do you do?

*You propose doing something that Jesus does not want!*

Peter wanted to build a temple so he and others could go back and repeat that mountain top experience whenever they wanted or needed it.

Peter may have been well intentioned but his agenda was NOT Christ's agenda. In fact, it was so far from Christ's agenda that Jesus told them not to tell anyone about the entire experience; not even the other disciples!

> *As they were coming down the mountain, Jesus instructed them, "Don't tell anyone what you have seen, until the Son of Man has been raised from the dead."* [Matthew 17:9, NIV]

> *As they were coming down the mountain, Jesus gave them orders not to tell anyone what they had seen until the Son of Man had risen from the dead.* [Mark 9:9, NIV]

The greatest mountaintop experience in Scripture led the greatest disciple on record to suggest the wrong thing to do!

Or let's look at what might be the second greatest mountaintop experience in Scripture; this one in the Old Testament and in this one Elijah was not a secondary character.

In I Kings, we can read the story of the first time Elijah was on earth. Starting in chapter seventeen, we see Elijah introduced at the time he was called by God to denounce the most evil king the Jews ever had.

> *And Ahab son of Omri did evil in the sight of the Lord above all before him. As if it had been a light thing for Ahab to walk in the sins of Jeroboam son of Nebat, he took for a wife Jezebel daughter of Ethbaal King of the Sidonians, and served Baal and worshiped him.* [I Kings 16:30-31, AMP]

Not only was Ahab the most evil king the Jews ever had, he married the most evil woman the Jews had ever known! And they both worshiped the most evil god the world had ever seen!

And God called Elijah to denounce Ahab and tell him that God was sending a drought to Israel because of what Ahab was doing. And Elijah did exactly what God asked and actually survived it!

Talk about a rush!

Then God put Elijah in the witness protection program and told Elijah to hide in a cave by the brook called Cherith east of Jordan.

After many months, the brook dried up. After all, there was a drought going on, right? So God gave him a new address and Elijah moved to a small town called Zerepath. There he met a woman who was a widow, with a child and who was starving because of the drought Elijah had called down. Elijah asked for some food and she told him she had almost nothing for herself and her son. Elijah told her that if she fed him God would make sure she would not starve. She could have said, *"Right!"* and walked away. But she decided to trust God and did what Elijah asked. As a result of her faith, God fed her and her son "for many days" until the rains came and everyone had food, as it says in chapter 17.

Then something horrible happened: the woman's son got sick and died. You know she had to be thinking, *"Oh yes, God promised that my son and I would not starve, so he let my son die of a fever."* But Elijah was still walking in the excitement and knowledge of God, and he took the son away to the attic room where Elijah slept. There he prayed and the son lived again. And Elijah lived in peace with the widow and her son until the rains came.

Sometime after raising the boy from the dead, on toward the end of the third year of the drought, God told Elijah to go back to Ahab and tell him it was about to rain. So Elijah and Ahab met, and Ahab was not at all in a good mood.

*When Ahab saw Elijah, Ahab said to him, "Are you he who troubles Israel?"* [I Kings 18:17, AMP]

I am certain that Elijah responded with, *"You haven't seen trouble yet. But trouble sure is coming!"* I haven't found any translation which includes that comment, but I am sure Elijah said it. Be that as it may (or may not), we do know what Elijah said in response.

*Elijah replied, "I have not troubled Israel, but you have, and your father's house, by forsaking the commandments of the Lord and by following the Baals."* [I Kings 18:18, AMP]

And Elijah issued a challenge. He told Ahab to gather 450 prophets of Baal (who Ahab followed) and the 400 prophets of the sex goddess Asherah (who Jezebel followed), along with all the people, and bring everyone to Mount Carmel.

Once there, Elijah put together a rigged demonstration; rigged against Elijah and his God. The 450 prophets of Baal, assisted by the 400 prophets of Asherah, set up an alter of stone with wood on it and a bull, fully cut up and prepared, placed on top. And then this 850 prophets of foreign gods were given all day long, from early morning to late afternoon, to pray down fire on the sacrifice.

And nothing happened. Except for Elijah laughing at them and taunting them and making public fools of them.

Then Elijah built his alter and prepared his sacrifice. Further, he asked that four large water jars be emptied on the alter; and again; and a third time. After twelve large water jars had been emptied on his alter, Elijah prayed 63 words. Not twelve hours, but less than one minute. And then fire came down from heaven and consumed everything: the sacrifice, the wood, the stones, the dust, even the water that had drained off the alter and into the trench surrounding the alter.

*When all the people saw it, they fell on their faces and they said, "The Lord, he is God! The Lord, he is God!"* [I Kings18:39, AMP]

I mean, ya think?

With the people properly motivated (and intimidated!), Elijah had them kill all the false prophets of Baal and Asherah.

And then Elijah prayed for rain, and it rained.

Something that is seldom mentioned in sermons and teachings on this event involves everyone leaving Mount Carmel before it rained. Elijah said something like, *"King Ahab, I am about to ask God to empty the clouds and have it rain all over us. You better get down the mountainside before the roads get so wet that your chariots won't be able to stay on the roads."* So Ahab headed down the mountain while Elijah prayed. After praying, but before the rain started, Elijah headed down the mountain himself. But Elijah was so excited and so motivated by his *"mountaintop experience"* that he ran all twenty miles back to town and got there before Ahab and his chariot.

### How was that for mountaintop excitement?

But no sooner than Ahab told Jezebel about everything, including the loss of the 400 prophets of her god that she used as personal servants, than Jezebel sent a message to Elijah: *"I am going to make you as dead as you made my prophets, and by this time tomorrow."* See I Kings 19:2.

And no matter how his mountaintop experience affected him, and no matter how excited he was about serving God under miraculous circumstances, Elijah allowed his emotions to take control, and...

*Elijah was afraid, and ran for his life.* [I Kings 19:3, NIVI

So what can we take away from a short review of two important, even awesome, mountaintop experiences? There are perhaps any number of lessons or conclusions we can draw from these two experiences, but I suspect that most would make for poor theology. However, I do believe we can draw two valid and valuable principles from these two Scriptural events.

*First, mountaintop experiences do not impart spiritual maturity or spiritual wisdom.*

*Second, mountaintop experiences feed our emotions, and emotions are seldom logical or wise.*

I do not believe that I err when I suggest that a mountaintop experience will often lead to a significant spiritual challenge, even a spiritual setback. Think about it.

In both of these biblical experiences, we see the people's emotions in control of them and unwise, even *wrong*, decisions that come out of these emotions. Peter wanted to build three temples so he could continue, or repeat continuously whenever he wanted, that wonderful experience. And Jesus not only wouldn't let him do it, Jesus wouldn't even let him _talk_ about it. And Elijah was so excited about God's victories that after seeing God's fire consume his sacrifice, after facing 850 enemy prophets and killing them all, even after outrunning Ahab's chariot for twenty miles, he runs and hides from one woman's threat.

When our emotions are running high, our emotions often make our decisions for us. And emotional decisions are often not based on the Word of God. When we react to what we see and hear and FEEL, it is our emotions that are in control of us and not the Spirit of God.

*We live by faith, not by sight.* [II Corinthians 5:7, NIV]

Or even more clearly translated:

*For we walk by faith [we regulate our lives and conduct ourselves by our conviction or belief respecting man's relationship to God and divine things, with trust and holy fervor; thus we walk] not by sight or appearance.* [I Corinthians 5:7, AMP]

So, are mountaintop experiences, are Christian pep rallies, *wrong*?

Absolutely not!

But if we NEED them, if we COUNT on these experiences to maintain a walk with God, if the emotional high is necessary for us to feel close to God and stay committed to following Jesus, then we need to recognize the FACT that we are Soil Type Two, from the parable in Chapter Four of Mark. We need to admit that we receive the Word of God with joy and excitement, but it doesn't take much to stifle our walk with God, or sidetrack our walk entirely. We need to take steps to strengthen our faith and our commitment so we can survive these simple and frequent challenges to our life in Christ. We need to develop the discipline inherent in the word "disciple" and from which the word is derived.

How?

*For this reason I kneel before the Father, from whom his whole family in heaven and on earth derives its name. I pray that out of his glorious riches he may strengthen you with power through his Spirit in your inner being, so that Christ may dwell in your hearts through faith. And I pray that you, being rooted and established in love, may have power, together with all the saints, to grasp how wide and long and high and deep is the love of Christ, and to know this love that surpasses knowledge - that you be filled to the measure of all the fullness of God.* [Ephesians 3:14-1 9, NIV]

In other words, *USE* those emotions. Use those emotions to drive you into God's Word, to make you want his Word, to make you thrill at the things his Holy Spirit leads you to learn and apply. Feed and strengthen your heart so that your love is more stable and more consistent. Allow God to turn your feelings into a new creation, a never before existing love for Jesus that is as strong and predictable as God's love for us.

We need to exchange our natural love for the love that comes from God and is focused on God and points us continuously and forever toward God.

More specifically, we need to move our eyes from *our love for Jesus* and put our eyes on *his love for us*. As long as our eyes are on our love for Jesus, we will look for any opportunities to feel that love and to express that love. When we cannot FEEL love for Jesus, we will lose sight of the FACT of *his love for us.* If we don't FEEL our love for Jesus, we will tend to question his love for us, and to feel distant from him. And then we will tend to seek out mountaintop experiences to help us FEEL our love for God. This will tend to make us dependent on those mountaintop experiences.

**But if we keep our eyes on his love for us, then our love for him will be a natural response to his love for us. And a natural response to his constant love for us will be <u>a more consistent love for him</u>.**

It is natural for us to be aware of and to experience our emotions. But it is spiritually immature for us to allow our emotions to drive our relationship with God. We MUST keep in the forefront of our minds *God's love for us*, and the constant and eternal nature of that love, or we will waver and fluctuate in *our love for him*. It MUST be his nature that provides the foundation for our relationship with him, and NOT our natures.

A mountaintop experience tends to move our eyes from God's love for us to our love for him; from his constant and eternal love for us to our fluctuating and temporal love for him. And if our eyes are on our fluctuating and temporal feelings for him, as soon as that mountaintop experience is over, we are particularly exposed to Satan's deceptions. That makes our mountaintop experiences a danger to our walks with God. Remember, the higher we get, the farther we can fall.

But when God's love permeates and saturates our hearts, we will see wisdom come from our emotions. When God's constant and consistent love for us is the "solid as a rock" foundation of our walk with him, we will see a stronger and more stable walk with God after all our mountaintop experiences. We will see God change our lives and the lives of others around us. And we will watch God change us from Soil Type Two to Soil Type Four in that parable.

**<u>And then we can totally enjoy and benefit from our Christian pep rallies.</u>**

Now, when is the next *Carmen* concert?

# WARNING!!!

## *Mountaintop Experience Ahead!*

Mountaintop Experiences produce high levels of excitement. High levels of excitement reduce our natural sense of caution. Walking on the edge of a sheer cliff does not seem so scary when on a spiritual high. If you believe you can fly, you are not so concerned about falling.

Keeping your spiritual guard up is most important when coming off a spiritual high or a mountaintop experience. Keep your eyes on God and allow the Holy Spirit to guide your steps. Only in this way can you avoid tumbling off the cliff.

Enjoy your mountaintop experiences, but recognize them for what they are – a serious opportunity for you to make unwise and emotional decisions or to rely on your feelings in order to walk with God.

Don't be a spiritual junkie where your feelings need constant feeding. Instead, feed your **spirit** with the Word of God and the fellowship of the Saints.

*We have so much to say about this, but it is hard to explain because you are slow to learn. In fact, though by this time you ought to be teachers, you need someone to teach you the elementary truths of God's Word all over again. You need milk, not solid food. Anyone who lives on milk, being still an infant, is not acquainted with the teaching about righteousness. But solid food is for the mature, who by constant use have trained themselves to distinguish good from evil. Therefore, let us leave the elementary teachings about Christ and go on to maturity...*
[Hebrews 5:11-6:1, NIV]

# ADDENDUM C

## *An Essay for Soil Type Three*

One of the weaknesses of Soil Type Three people is the overwhelming nature of the concern for the circumstances of life. A subtle but very common cause of this concern is the need for a reason, for an explanation, for all the negative circumstances in life. If these people cannot find an acceptable reason for the negatives in life, they begin to doubt God and his love for them. And if they *CAN* find a reason, they somehow believe that knowledge will help them avoid the negatives in life. Finding no reason at all for the negatives is taken as a sign that God cannot be counted on to love us or to honor all his many promises to Believers. This can sometimes cause these people to become overly concerned with their accomplishments in life and especially in the name of God. Unconsciously, they believe that the more good things they can do, the more bad things in life they can avoid. *If they can discern the REASON for the circumstances, they can figure out WHAT TO DO next time to avoid those circumstances.* So these people sometimes become consumed with the need to do *everything possible* that can be considered good in God's eyes. And this almost manic perspective *on* life can lead these people to attempt too much *in* life. With too many tasks on their plates, they simply cannot keep up with everything. Hence, they often get bogged down and can accomplish few tasks well or perform them to completion. This essay addresses their need to have an explanation for everything that drives these people to try to accomplish too much.

# *Christian Fatalism*

I hear the question/issue almost every day: *"What is God trying to teach me by by putting me through these circumstances?"* Or maybe, *"…by sending me to prison?"* Or maybe *"...by giving me a flat tire?"* Or maybe *"...by having me get fired?"*

First, personally, I don't believe that God sent me to prison. Second, personally, I don't think that God sent me to prison because he couldn't teach me some specific lesson in any other way. Third, generally, I really don't believe that Scripture teaches that God sends bad things or hard times to teach people lessons. Fourth, generally, God often sends Believers into circumstances (good AND bad) to be in place for someone else's need or benefit.

First, I don't believe that God sent me to prison. I believe that I started on a path back in 1990 which had the risk of getting negative attention from the IRS. As soon as I started helping others fight the IRS, I was in danger. I thought about that a lot before launching. My wife and I prayed about it a lot. And we both concluded certain facts: that we must follow this course of action, that it was to benefit others who could not help themselves, that it was legal and lawful, and that it was our only option if we wanted to maintain our integrity after studying the issues as much as we studied them. At that time, I believed that the greatest risk was a felony conviction resulting in 5-8 years in prison for me, but no prison time for Bonnie. We decided to move ahead and run that risk back in 1990. It was our decision, and my actions, that resulted in me being in prison. God did not send me there; a dishonest prosecutor and an ineffective defense sent me there.

Second, I don't think God sent me (or anyone) to prison to teach me (or us) something that he could not have taught me (or us) on the outside. It is an easy thing to predict in advance or perceive after the fact certain actions or behaviors that will result from prison influences, and it would be an easy thing to cling to one or more of them as explanation for my going to prison. It would probably be impossible to choose one of those actions or results and claim with confidence and spiritual authority that _THIS_ is why God sent me to prison, but I could select several of the perceived benefits, or even all of them, and claim that they were why God sent me here. Most people would

144

make a list of all positive results of being in prison, and refer to that list as answer to the above question.

*Most people HAVE to have a logical explanation for their bad circumstances in life to which they can point in order to maintain their faith in the love and goodness of God.*

But think about it, folks. Job was going through life enjoying EVERYTHING because EVERYTHING was awesome. Then God bumped into Satan at the mall and bragged about Job to Satan. And then Satan set about destroying Job's life. When Satan was finished taking Job's health and everything good away from him, and Job asked God "*Why?*" God NEVER answered Job and NEVER justified allowing Satan to destroy Job. Look again at Scripture. There was NOTHING Job needed to learn, yet his life was destroyed anyway. Perhaps the only thing Job learned by going through his horrible circumstances was the fact that God had the right to do anything he darn well pleases with and to any of us. But anyone who points that out to us scares the crap out of all of us, and paints God as being a mean and vicious God.

Of course, we like to remember the last part of Job's life where things were better than they ever were before. We like that because it allows us to hope that if we go through anything like Job did, well, at least things would be better after all the dust settled and the blood dried.

But there was no lesson for Job to learn; there was nothing God wanted to teach Job that required such destruction and pain. I mean, read the first 3 verses of Job again:

*"This man was blameless and upright; he feared God and shunned evil... He was the greatest man among all the people of the East."* [Job 1:1-3, in part, NIV]

Job was blameless before God, and then Job went through hell.

Most people claim that Job had too much pride and needed to learn a lesson. I believe that such claims are based in ignorance and the *NEED TO FIND A REASON*.  Please notice that it was not Job who claimed "he was the greatest man among all the people of the earth" which has been claimed by many -- it was the narrator of the story who made that claim as he was describing Job.  Scripture gives no evidence at all of any sin in Job's life, and no evidence at all of a need to be taught any lessons.

Third, I don't believe Scripture teaches that God sends bad things or bad circumstances into the lives of Believers to teach them spiritual truths.  There may be many good things that Believers learn when they experience bad events and bad circumstances, but I see no passage that claims this as one of God's teaching tools.

In fact, I see just the opposite.  Bad things happen. Period.

> *"He causes his sun to rise on the evil and the good, and sends the rain on the righteous and the unrighteous."*
> [Matthew 5:45, NIV]

> *"...for he maketh his sun to rise on the evil and on the good, and sendeth rain on the just and on the unjust."*
> [Matthew 5:45, KJV]

> *"...for He causes His sun to rise on the evil and the good, and sends rain on the righteous and the unrighteous."*
> [Matthew 5:45, NASB]

### Bad things happen!

Sometimes those bad things come from God.  And no amount of positive thinking or self-help is going to remove a really bad day when that really bad day is sent by God.  Further, no amount of lessons learned will take that bad day away.

### But most Christians NEED to see a reason for bad things or bad circumstances!

Most Christians NEED to believe that God has a reason behind the horrors in their lives in order to for them to continue in faith, believing in a loving and gracious God!  Most Christians today would NEVER survive Job's experience! Most Christians today would follow the advice of one of Job's friends to *"Curse God and die!"*

It is hard or even impossible for most Christians to believe that God would allow bad things to happen without making them better. It is even more difficult for them to believe that God just might *SEND* bad things.

Fourth, God sometimes sends Believers into bad circumstances to have them in place for the benefit of someone else. Remember, Paul commented once that it would be better for him to go home to heaven, but it would be better for others that he remain on this earth in difficult circumstances. So Paul chose to remain for the benefit of others.. Remember, in the Garden, Jesus just plain didn't want to go through with the whole crucifixion thing, including being separated from his Father. Yet he submitted to it because of the unbelievable benefit to the entire world.

I have learned to say each morning as I awake: *"I am but a pawn in God's Great Chess game. I wonder what move he has for me today!"* I have learned that living this way allows for each day to be exciting and fulfilling, regardless of being in prison; regardless of *ANY* circumstances! And I have also learned that sometimes pawns get sacrificed.

But, as Paul said in Romans:

*"And we know that in all things God works for the good of those who love him, who have been called according to his purpose."* [Romans 8:28, NIV]

*And we know that all things work together for good to them that love God, to them who are the called according to his purpose.* [Romans 8:28, KJV]

It does not say that God *CAUSES* ALL THINGS; it says that God *causes all things to work together* for our good and his glory. Sometimes that means the Father causes my circumstances to work together for my good. Sometimes that means he causes my circumstances to work together for the benefit of someone else. No matter what, SOMEONE gains eternal benefits from my circumstances. I can live with that!

The question is not *"What should I learn here?"* but *"How can I be used here?"*

And God has used me greatly in prison in ways that are very exciting, and I will always treasure my time spent here.

No, I will *NEVER* like prison! No I will *NEVER* believe that I deserved coming here or my prison sentence. No, I will *NEVER* believe that prison was a good thing for me.

**But I will always treasure the opportunities I have had to touch the lives of men who are hurting and struggling and trying to see God in all of this.**

And there are a lot of Believers here in prison; some preachers, some Bible College professors, some sincere Christians who just don't know how God could allow them to go to prison when they believe they were innocent, and ESPECIALLY many men who believe that God no longer has a use for them and has discarded them.

And I have had the privilege and the thrill and the honor of talking with these men and of helping them to see how God still wants to use them, and of helping them grow in ALL their life circumstances.

There are too many examples in Scripture to mention all of them; of good people going through bad experiences with no clear explanation from God. If we go back to Daniel, we see that he believed God *COULD* keep him alive, but <u>NOT</u> that God *WOULD* keep him alive. I believe that Scripture indicates that Daniel expected to die that day, and he was at peace with it. When God finally DID keep him alive, Daniel gave God the credit for his miracle and received a job promotion! Undoubtedly, God keeping Daniel alive got people's attention. But if you read the entire story again carefully, you will see that it was Daniel's *attitude* all through the process (as well as all through his captivity) that so impressed the Chaldean ruler that

Daniel was promoted after he partied with some lions and angels.

Something similar happened to Shadrach, Meshach, and Abednego. They suffered a death sentence and survived, and that got them attention. I believe Scripture indicates the men believed they were going to die that day, and they faced it with godly attitudes. And a careful reading of the passage shows that it was their *attitudes,* that day and all through their captivity, which got them promotions and made their lives better.

They were (all 4 of them) cast in very bad circumstances, and they were (all 4 of them) manifesting an attitude of loving and serving and worshiping God through it all.

**And they were (all 4 of them) NEVER given an explanation by God!**

God wanted that attitude more than anything. And when they survived their death sentences, did God free them and allow them to go home? No. But God did give them promotions and other benefits.

**God used their hearts, shown by their attitudes, to touch other people's lives!**

I am convinced that God is not situational in his perspective, but attitudinal. What I mean is, God is less concerned about our circumstances than he is about our attitudes *IN* our circumstances. It takes the supernatural grace of God to face bad circumstances with the right attitudes. And it is those right attitudes that affect the hearts and lives of those around us.

Yes, surviving a death sentence gets attention. But that only sells tickets. It is the heartfelt attitude of *"Yet though he slay me, I will still serve him"* which Job showed that touches hearts and brings people to God.

God is more concerned that I face each day as his Ambassador, ready for his use, than he is that I am in prison serving an unjustified sentence. I may have to deal with being in prison, but it is in being in prison that I get the joy of touching the lives of these men.

**WHERE I am is merely SO THAT God can use me in the life of someone here!**

# ADDENDUM D

## *An Essay for Soil Type Four*

Soil Type Four people tend to be very zealous in their pursuit of God to the extent that they can become consumed by that very zeal. When this happens, they often take their eyes off the joy of experientially knowing God and place their eyes on increasing their collections of facts ABOUT God or their many accomplishments FOR God. Often, when this happens, their pursuit of God can easily become driven by their desire for facts and lose sight of living in the power of God's Holy Spirit. Taking their eyes off God becomes an "occupational hazard" and that will always result in a powerless life. The following essay addresses one of the tactics of keeping your eyes on God as you pursue life and godliness.

# *THE MINISTRY OF THE HOLY SPIRIT*
John 16: 8-11

I would like us to take a look at a passage in the Bible that almost certainly you have heard, possibly read, and maybe even studied, in the past. Most likely you have made reference to this passage (or at least what you believe this passage to mean) dozens, if not hundreds, of times in your desire and attempt to grow in your spiritual life.

We have all heard so many comments and even many sermons based on what people believe this passage means that many of us have stopped thinking about the actual words that are there. This "accept without thought" in Believers is a pattern throughout history which often leads to diluted theology, which itself leads to diluted effectiveness and spiritual frustration. I believe it does so again in this passage.

*For I can testify about them that they are zealous for God, but their zeal is not based on knowledge.* [Romans 10:2, NIV]

So let us see if we can perhaps glean further truth from this passage that might help us avoid this pattern of setback and failure.

But first, think about hiking a mountain trail. I know that the most difficult hike many of you experience takes you from one store to another in the local mall. But think about hiking a mountain trail anyway, and let's see if we can find something here to use in our spiritual journeys.

You are high on a mountainside with trees all around you. Suddenly, the trail breaks through the trees and you see a deep valley on your left and a steep rise into more mountain on your right. The trail ahead of you narrows to just a few feet wide edging a near vertical drop into the valley below. The trail is well-established, so you conclude that it must be safe. Still, the steep drop-off fills you with more than just caution.

You look for handholds and you see none. You think about it and conclude that a level path three feet wide is safe enough for you to pass without problems. After all, you remind yourself, you walk down sidewalks at home all the time without stumbling or falling off, and this path is just as wide so it must surely be passable.

Yet you cannot help but look down at the valley floor several hundred feet below. You even lean out and peer over the cliff to get a better view or to see if there might be a shelf or something to catch you if you should fall. Each step forward brings a greater fear of losing your footing and falling over the abrupt edge.

Then, maybe a hundred feet in front of you, where the trail turns away from the cliff on the left into a small field with a few trees that seems to be almost level, you see your hiking partner. He is calling to you. "Don't look down," he shouts. "Look at me and walk towards me."

Relieved, you look away from almost certain death. Watching him carefully, you walk another twenty feet, looking intently in his face. And you are surprised at how easy it is to walk in the center of the path, almost as if there is no cliff just inches from your left foot.

Then, you are distracted by the "*scree*" of an eagle in the distance. You look out to the next mountain in search of the eagle, and your eyes fall to the valley that separates you from that mountain. Looking deep into that valley, you see the cliff at your feet and immediately fear the deadly fall you are about to experience. For a moment, you are dizzy as you peer over the edge. You lean even farther over the precipice. Then you suddenly experience such vertigo that you feel yourself about to fall into the void. Fear strikes at your heart, taking control of your feet. Your knees become rubber. You step even closer to that which you fear so much.

"Don't look down! Look at me!" You realize your hiking buddy is still shouting at you, almost screaming at you.

Your eyes lift from the deep chasm below, and the fall you are about to experience, and your eyes raise to the concerned face of your friend. Mere seconds before you step into the void, you instead walk toward your hiking partner. Just hearing the voice of your friend takes away the fear. The very act of walking toward your friend takes you away from the dangerous edge.

Each time you look down into the deep valley, you get closer to falling over the edge. And each time you look back at the face of your partner, you find it easy to remain on the path. After many cycles of looking down and then looking up, you realize that it is so much easier to look up. Walking is simpler, safer, when you look up at your hiking partner. You ask yourself, "Why look down and run the risk of falling when all I have to do is look up?" The answer seems so obvious.

After all, looking up is so easy to do!

Then you look down again and the answer seems to dissipate into the thin air you fear.

***This is the ministry of the Holy Spirit with Believers: <u>he calls us to look up</u>. He calls us to do exactly what we know to do, but simply need reminding from time to time.***

Each time we see that valley, with its distant floor and the rocks scattered around it, we walk closer to the edge. We don't mean to; we don't want to. But we do. And each time we look down at our sin, at our failures, at what we know in our hearts we should never do but seem to do it anyway, we increase the chance of walking back into that sin. Sometimes sin just looks fascinating, and maybe even attractive!

Yet each time we look at the face of Jesus, we find it is a simple task to walk in the path he calls us to walk.

Does the Holy Spirit call out to us and say, "Look at the valley and don't fall into it?" No, not at all. Never! The Holy Spirit is constantly calling out to us, "Look at Jesus. Keep your eyes on his face, and you will always be able to walk in his path."

Again, this is the ministry of the Holy Spirit with Believers: to point us to Jesus and his righteousness so we can more easily walk in that righteousness like he wants us to do.

Is this a nice story, designed to make us feel better? Is this a new theology that tends to make us focus on simplistic answers and pop psychology rather than the reality all around us? Is this a cheap technique designed to help us navigate through the often dangerous and difficult minefield of life?

Or is this a map through that minefield, drawn by the Creator to make it easier for us to walk down his path?

Is it better to look down and hope we don't walk off that cliff? Or is it better to look up at our Guide and know where to walk?

Let's take a closer look at the Bible and see what it says about this issue. Turn to the Sixteenth Chapter of the Gospel of

John, starting with the eighth verse and continuing through the eleventh verse.

> *When he comes, he will convict the world of guilt in regards to sin, righteousness, and judgment; in regards to sin, because men do not believe in me; in regards to righteousness, because I am going to the Father, where you can see me no longer; in regard to judgment, because the prince of this world now stands condemned.* [John 16:8-11, NIV]

> *And when he comes, he will reprove the world of sin, righteousness, and judgment; of sin, because they believe not on me; of righteousness, because I go to my Father and ye see me no more; of judgment, because the prince of this world is judged.* [John 16:8-11, KJV]

In this passage, Jesus tells us why it was important for him to die here on earth and enter back into heaven -- so the Holy Spirit can come to men in a new way and with a specific ministry that will benefit everyone.

Jesus further tells us that the Holy Spirit has three functions on earth, depending on the recipients of that ministry.

The first group of recipients is *unbelievers*. The ministry of the Holy Spirit to unbelievers is to *convict* or *reprove* or sometimes translated into *correct* unbelievers of their sin. The Greek word used here is addressing the *state of sinfulness*, and not individual acts of sin, or individual transgressions.

**With unbelievers, the Holy Spirit shows them their need of Jesus.**

This calls into question sermons against alcohol, or drugs, or infidelity, or pornography, or all of the many subjects and topics of our evangelical efforts aimed at convincing unbelievers to switch directions and follow Jesus. Perhaps there is value in these efforts, but Jesus here seems to say that the Holy Spirit doesn't do that, and is only involved with unbelievers to the extent that he points to their need for Jesus. I find no other function spoken of by Jesus where the Holy Spirit interacts with unbelievers. He seems to be concerned with pointing them to Jesus, convicting them of their need for Jesus, and nothing else.

The second group that is the focus of efforts by the Holy Spirit is *Believers*. His ministry with us is to convict or reprove or correct Believers concerning the righteousness of Christ. In so doing, we can see more clearly where to walk and how to live. Jesus is no longer physically with us so we can no longer watch how he lives and moves and acts and touches lives. Therefore, the Holy Spirit has to constantly draw us back to what we have already seen and heard and learned about how we should live and move and act and touch others, as written in his Word.

With Believers, the Holy Spirit shows us the righteousness of Jesus, so we can walk in it more easily and more consistently.

I have yet to read where Jesus or any biblical writer tells us that the Holy Spirit points *Believers* to their sins, or to their failures, or to the short but terrible victories that Satan wins in their lives. According to Jesus, as recorded in the 16th Chapter of John, the Holy Spirit does not seem to convict Believers of individual sins or transgressions, but he instead points us toward the life of Jesus for an example of how to live and respond to others. It is in seeing Jesus and his righteousness that we become aware of how we have failed him, and it is only in seeing Jesus and his righteousness that we can keep our eyes on him and not look down or behind us to the path where we stumble so close to the edge.

**With Believers, the Holy Spirit shows us where to walk, not what to avoid.**

*For we walk by faith, not by sight.* [II Corinthians 5:7, NIV]

It is Satan who tricks us into looking at the sin, falsely telling us we can avoid stepping in it if we focus on it, if we rebuke ourselves for stepping in it in the past, and if we see the edges of sin clearly enough that we can step ever closer to sin without actually stepping in it. We can avoid this deceptive trap by reminding Satan that he has already lost the war, and then, without looking down at the path at our feet, we turn to Jesus and look into his face, where we can see love and forgiveness and righteousness; where we can see where to walk.

Does it really matter if the Holy Spirit points us at our sins, or points us to the holiness and righteousness of Jesus? Think about it for a few minutes, allowing the Holy Spirit to speak to you.

The more we allow the Holy Spirit to minister to us by reminding us to look into the face of Jesus and see his righteousness, the easier it will be to walk in his path. The more we allow Satan to focus our attention on the sins we have committed or we might again commit, the easier it is for Satan to get us to look over the edge, down into the valley where the rocks await our failures.

Tony Robbins is not the only one to tell us to look up and see the positive things in life. The Holy Spirit tells us to look up, see Jesus and his righteousness, and we WILL walk in his path – we WILL receive power to walk like Jesus walked!

*For the law of the Spirit of Life in Christ Jesus hath made me free from the law of sin and death.* [Romans 8:2, KJV]

*...because through Christ Jesus the law of the Spirit of life set me free from the law of sin and death.* [Romans 8:2, NIV]

Spiritually speaking, we walk where we are looking. We can have "victory in Jesus" only if we see Jesus before us. And it is the Holy Spirit's job to point us to Jesus at all times. When we are looking at our "hiking partner" it is a simple thing to walk in the middle of the path. But when we see the edge of the cliff, when we see our past failures, when we see where we MIGHT walk, we will usually get dizzy with Satan's lies and tricks, and walk off that cliff once again.

*There is therefore no condemnation to them which are in Christ Jesus, who walk not after the flesh, but after the Spirit.* [Romans 8:1, KJV]

*Therefore, there is now no condemnation for those who are in Christ Jesus.*
[Romans 8:1, NIV]

When we keep our eyes on Jesus, the author and finisher of our faith, we can and will walk in the path he has laid out for us.

*Therefore as you have received Christ Jesus the Lord, so walk in Him.* [Colossians 2:6, NASB]

But whatever things were gain to me, those things I have counted as loss for the sake of Christ. More than that, I count all things to be loss in view of the surpassing value of knowing Christ Jesus my Lord, for whom I have suffered the loss of all things, and count them but rubbish so that I may gain Christ, and may be found in Him, not having a righteousness of my own derived from the Law, but that which is through faith in Christ, the righteousness which comes from God on the basis of faith, that I may know Him and the power of His resurrection and the fellowship of His sufferings, being conformed to His death; in order that I may attain to the resurrection from the dead. Not that I have already obtained it or have already become perfect, but I press on so that I may lay hold of that for which also I was laid hold of by Christ Jesus. Brethren, I do not regard myself as having laid hold of it yet; but one thing I do: forgetting what lies behind and reaching forward to what lies ahead, I press on toward the goal for the prize of the upward call of God in Christ Jesus. [Philippians 3:7-14, NASB]

Other books and articles by this author
Available on Amazon's Kindle Library:


# In the series <u>Short Theologies</u>:


**Does God Sentence People to an Eternity of Punishment in Hell?**
Can a Loving God Punish People?
(<u>Short Theologies</u> – Book 1)


**Did Jesus Claim to be God?**
(<u>Short Theologies</u> – Book 2)


**Predestination**
Another View of What Scripture Teaches
<u>Short Theologie</u>s – Book 3)


**WATER BAPTISM**
When and Why
(<u>Short Theologies</u> –Book 4)


**A Discussion of the Role of Elders in the Local Church**
Do Elders Rule?
(<u>Short Theologies</u> – Book 5)


**Women's Rights In The Bible**
Must Women Submit to Men?
(<u>Short Theologies</u> – Book 6)

**The Ministry of the Holy Spirit**
John 18:8-11
(*Short Theologies* – Book 7)


**Judging Others**
"Who Am I To Judge?"
(Short Theologies – Book 8)


**Christian Fatalism**
"Everything is for a purpose"
(*Short Theologies* – Book 9)


**Salvation**
What is it?  And How Do You Get It?
(Short Theologies – Book 10)


**Mountaintop Experiences**
Pursuing Spiritual Highs
(Short Theologies -- Book 11)


**Jesus Declares War**
Pharisees Beware!
(Short Theologies – Book 12)


**Eternal Salvation**
The Biblical Purpose For Salvation


**Inductive Bible Study**
A Simple Bible Study Technique

## Political Fiction:

*(Series <u>Revolution</u>)*

**Revolution**
Shattering the Republic
*(<u>Revolution!</u> – Book 1)*


## Political Non-Fiction:

**Patriotism v. Nationalism**
The Aftermath of 09/11


**Master File**
What do IRS secret files on you actually say about you?


**Federal Jurisdiction**
What Powers does the Federal Government have within the
Several States?


**Rights and Government**
Are Individual Rights Compatible With Government?


**The Christian's Response to Political Activism**